Trade Union Cooperation in Europe

Bengt Furåker · Bengt Larsson

Trade Union Cooperation in Europe

Patterns, Conditions, Issues

Bengt Furåker
Department of Sociology
and Work Science
University of Gothenburg
Gothenburg, Sweden

Bengt Larsson
Department of Sociology
and Work Science
University of Gothenburg
Gothenburg, Sweden

ISBN 978-3-030-38769-3   ISBN 978-3-030-38770-9 (eBook)
https://doi.org/10.1007/978-3-030-38770-9

© The Editor(s) (if applicable) and The Author(s) 2020. This book is an open access publication.
Open Access This book is licensed under the terms of the Creative Commons Attribution 4.0 International License (http://creativecommons.org/licenses/by/4.0/), which permits use, sharing, adaptation, distribution and reproduction in any medium or format, as long as you give appropriate credit to the original author(s) and the source, provide a link to the Creative Commons license and indicate if changes were made.
The images or other third party material in this book are included in the book's Creative Commons license, unless indicated otherwise in a credit line to the material. If material is not included in the book's Creative Commons license and your intended use is not permitted by statutory regulation or exceeds the permitted use, you will need to obtain permission directly from the copyright holder.
The use of general descriptive names, registered names, trademarks, service marks, etc. in this publication does not imply, even in the absence of a specific statement, that such names are exempt from the relevant protective laws and regulations and therefore free for general use.
The publisher, the authors and the editors are safe to assume that the advice and information in this book are believed to be true and accurate at the date of publication. Neither the publisher nor the authors or the editors give a warranty, expressed or implied, with respect to the material contained herein or for any errors or omissions that may have been made. The publisher remains neutral with regard to jurisdictional claims in published maps and institutional affiliations.

Cover illustration: © Harvey Loake

This Palgrave Pivot imprint is published by the registered company Springer Nature Switzerland AG
The registered company address is: Gewerbestrasse 11, 6330 Cham, Switzerland

Preface

We are grateful for the funding of two research projects, on which this book is based. The first was called *Can Trade Unions Within Europe Cooperate?* It was sponsored by the Swedish Council for Working Life and Social Research (FAS 2008–0246), for the period 2009–2011, with Bengt Furåker as principal investigator. The second project, which was a continuation of the first one, had the title *Conditions for and Obstacles to Trade Union Cooperation in Europe. A Comparative Study of Countries and Sectors.* It was headed by Bengt Larsson and funded by Riksbankens Jubileumsfond (RJ P13–0776:1), 2014–2016. We are also grateful for the additional grant that Riksbankens Jubileumsfond gave to finance Open Access publication of the book (RJ P13–0776:6 OA). During the course of our studies we have had several collaborators. Mattias Bengtsson and Kristina Lovén Seldén participated in both projects and Anton Törnberg and Patrik Vulkan were involved in the second one. We want to thank all of them for their great commitment and valuable contributions.

Gothenburg, Sweden
December 2019

Bengt Furåker
Bengt Larsson

Contents

1 **Why and How to Study Trade Union Cooperation in Europe?**   1
   Introduction   1
   Aim and Outline of the Book   3
   Trade Unions and Industrial Relations in Europe   6
      Comparisons of Industrial Relations in Europe   9
      Sectoral Comparisons across Europe   13
      European-Level Industrial Relations   14
      Sectoral European-Level Industrial Relations   16
   Data Collection Methods and Empirical Materials   19
      Quantitative Materials   20
      Qualitative Materials   22
   References   23

2 **Patterns of Transnational Trade Union Cooperation in Europe**   29
   Introduction   30
   Multilevel Structures of Cooperation   31

Cooperation within Meta-organizations	35
Networks of Bi- and Multilateral Cooperation	42
Forms of Cooperation	47
Channels for Influencing EU Policies	52
Focus and Topics of Cooperation	55
Obstacles to Cooperation	58
Factors Facilitating Cooperation	61
Cultural Obstacles to Cooperation	63
References	70

3 The European Trade Union Movement and the Issue of Statutory Minimum Wages — 75

Introduction	75
Statutory Minimum Wages in Europe: A Brief Background	76
Arguments for Legislated Minimum Wages	79
Arguments against Legislated Minimum Wages	82
What Do Survey Data Tell Us?	84
The Cleavage in the European Trade Union Movement	92
Conclusion	99
References	103

4 Revision of the EU Posting of Workers Directive, Social Dumping and Trade Unions' Position — 109

Introduction	110
What Do We Know about Posting of Workers in Europe?	112
Key Concepts	114
The Directives of 1996 and 2014	118
The European Commission's Proposal	119
Examples of Cross-Border Trade Union Rivalry and Cooperation	122
Do We Find an East–West Conflict over the Commission's Proposal?	126
Political Reactions	127
The Social Partners' Responses	128
Conclusion and Discussion	132
References	135

| 5 | Concluding Discussion | 141 |

Index 153

List of Figures

Fig. 2.1 Generalized map of a trade union cooperation structure 33
Fig. 2.2 Balance scores on own channels vs. cooperative channels, by region 55

List of Tables

Table 1.1	Industrial relations regimes in Europe	10
Table 1.2	Directives and agreements of cross-industry relevance	17
Table 1.3	Directives and agreements of sectoral relevance	19
Table 1.4	Information on survey 1 by region, 2010–2011	20
Table 1.5	Information on survey 2 by region, 2015–2016	21
Table 2.1	Trade unions' readiness to transfer authority to the ETUC	37
Table 2.2	Perceived importance of meta-organizations for trade union cooperation in the last 10 years	38
Table 2.3	Trade unions' agreement on various statements on the ESSD	41
Table 2.4	Intra- and cross-regional ties in trade union cooperation networks	46
Table 2.5	Participation in European trade union activities during the last three years	49
Table 2.6	Participation in specified forms of cooperation during the past five years	51
Table 2.7	Trade unions' channels of cooperation to influence EU policies	54

List of Tables

Table 2.8	Trade union cooperation on various topics during the past five years	57
Table 2.9	Perceived obstacles to trade union cooperation	59
Table 2.10	Factors considered important for trade unions' successful transnational cooperation	62
Table 3.1	Summary indicators on attitudes to minimum wage issues	86
Table 3.2	Degree of agreement with various statements on possible advantages of statutory minimum wages	89
Table 3.3	Degree of agreement with various statements on possible disadvantages of statutory minimum wages	90
Table 3.4	Degree of agreement with the statement 'ETUC should work for common European norms on minimum wages'	91

1

Why and How to Study Trade Union Cooperation in Europe?

Abstract This chapter gives a general background to the issue of transnational union cooperation in Europe and presents the aim, outline and delimitations of the book. It also pays attention to a number of concepts that can be relevant in the analysis of European trade unions and industrial relations. In this way, a theoretical context is provided for the analyses to come. There is moreover a rather detailed description of the empirical materials and methods used in the following chapters.

Keywords Transnational trade union cooperation · Industrial relations · Data collection methods

Introduction

Against the background of a gradually widening and deepening European integration process, transnational trade union cooperation is of great importance for workers. The trade union movement has traditionally a strong position in Europe compared to other regions of the world, but this strength is largely rooted in national industrial relations institutions. The increasing integration and enlargement of the European internal market have created challenges for labour organizations to enhance their cross-border coordination and collaboration, not to be marginalized in terms of influence when safeguarding the interests of their members (Erne 2008; Gajewska 2009; Gumbrell-McCormick and Hyman 2013; Seeliger 2019).

A problem in this connection is that national unions in Europe are experiencing setbacks due to declining membership numbers ('union density') and decreasing power resources (Kelly 2015; Lehndorff et al. 2017). This is partly related to the EU integration process, for example when the scope of action for unions at national level was reduced by the European Court of Justice's decisions in a series of notable judgements in the early 2000s, in particular the so-called *Laval Quartet* of rulings (Bücker and Warneck 2010). Moreover, in the aftermath of the economic crisis starting in 2008, the increased transnational governance of the Euro-zone countries within the EU brought widespread social consequences for workers. Parts of the austerity policy following the crisis led to a weakening of trade unions' power and negotiating opportunities in some countries, adding to the already existing pressures towards neo-liberalization and decentralization of collective bargaining at national level (Baccaro and Howell 2017; Marginson 2015).

The EU is sometimes depicted as a liberal market project, driven by 'negative integration', which means that the main project is to remove barriers to the free movement of goods, services, labour and capital (Scharpf 1996). However, there have also been many discussions and initiatives over the years to introduce and strengthen elements of 'positive integration', for example by shaping common identities, rights and conditions for citizens in Member States (Rhodes 2015). These ambitions are often referred to as the European 'social dimension' or even as 'social Europe' (Seeliger 2019: 28–31). One quite recent example is the *European Pillar of Social Rights* with its chapters setting up principles concerning 'Equal opportunities and access to the labour market'; 'Fair working conditions' and 'Social protection and inclusion' (European Commission 2017).

Cooperation between trade unions in Europe is actually since long supported and institutionalized by the European Commission as an integrated part of the EU multilevel governance system. The Commission has facilitated structures for unions and employer associations to participate in both consultations on EU policies and social dialogue. This offers possibilities of negotiating agreements that can be turned into directives (Rhodes 2015). Even though lately questioned by some unions and researchers (Tricart 2019), the Commission has repeatedly emphasized the importance of European-level social dialogue between trade unions and employer organizations for EU governance:

> Developing and fostering social dialogue is an essential element of the European social model, as it plays a crucial role in promoting competitiveness and fairness and enhancing economic prosperity and social well-being. European social dialogue complements the social dialogue happening at the national level. (European Commission 2016: 3)

Historically, the EU social dimension has been very much about employment and working life issues. To realize the European social model, a crucial condition is that the labour organizations are able to take an active role in safeguarding and advancing measures in the intended direction. If they are to do so, they must be able to cooperate effectively across national borders. This is especially difficult as union power is declining at national level in many countries, while simultaneously many important decisions are made in multinational companies and a lot of politics has moved beyond the national arena.

Aim and Outline of the Book

This book aims to provide an analysis of transnational trade union cooperation in Europe—its forms and focuses and its conditions and obstacles. It is not only a study of union cooperation as such, but also illustrates the interconnections between national and European industrial relations. Thereby it gives examples of the workings of the European integration process in the labour markets, and particularly of the potential and difficulties in developing and deepening the social dimension.

There are of course a number of limitations when we approach such broad issues in a narrow format; of course, not everything of relevance can be covered. As economic and political conditions change fast both nationally and in the EU, we have to hit a moving target in our analyses. Our empirical attention is mainly directed to cooperation between unions at sectoral and cross-sectoral level. Therefore we have less to say about the European structures of workers' collaboration at company level, established in the form of European Works Councils (EWCs), important as they may be. For this level of union cooperation, the reader has to search for other scholarly overviews (e.g., Hann et al. 2017; Whittall et al. 2007).

Since our focus is on trade union cooperation, we provide few details about the employer side and the European institutions as well as about the interaction between these two and the unions, possibly with some exception of Chapter 4. As we use broader scholarly research to place union collaboration within the context of European industrial relations, at least some anchor points are supplied for our analyses. The role of EU institutions as facilitators and driving forces of union cooperation has been covered in many useful overviews, on which we will lean (e.g., Rhodes 2015; Smismans 2012; Welz 2008). With respect to the employer side, there seem to be fewer studies, but there are quite a number of valuable overviews of the interactions between employers and trade unions in European-level social dialogues (e.g., Keller and Weber 2011; Perin and Léonard 2011; Prosser 2016; Tricart 2019).

Besides presenting the background and the aim of the book, this introductory chapter has two major subsections. The first introduces some main theoretical concepts and discusses different approaches to the study of European industrial relations. One strand is the comparative approach, which is usually about making comparisons between countries, between industrial relations regimes, or between sectors. Another dimension is the existence of a supranational European level, which can be scrutinized in terms of actors, institutions, interactions and outcomes. The current chapter ends with a description of the empirical materials used in the analyses in the book.

Chapter 2 gives an overview of the patterns of cross-border union cooperation based on our empirical studies. We begin with a brief discussion of the multilevel structures that exist in such collaboration and continue by presenting trade unions' views on the importance of working together at different levels and on the potential benefits to be gained through this. In the second section, we go into a more detailed discussion about what topics and themes that are important in transnational union cooperation and what forms of cooperation that are preferred in different sectors and industrial relations regimes. The last parts of Chapter 2 examine the most important obstacles and facilitators to union collaboration in Europe.

Then, in Chapter 3, we move to a more detailed analysis of an issue of great importance for trade unions: statutory minimum wages. It is a case study of union views regarding minimum wage legislation at national and European levels. After providing some basic information on such regulation in Europe, the analysis concentrates on different arguments for and against it. Empirical data, from surveys as well as from interviews and documents, are used to describe the positions taken by labour organizations. There is a deep cleavage on the topic in the European union movement and the resistance to legislation is strongest in the Nordic countries, whereas the opinion is much more positive in most other parts of Europe. The European Trade Unions Confederation (ETUC)—the unions' large cooperation organization in Europe—has thus had certain difficulties to deal with, but it has been able to find a compromise that its members can tolerate. Still, importantly, the issue of statutory minimum wages is not something that all European labour organizations can presently be expected to collaborate on.

Chapter 4 contains an analysis of another potentially divisive issue in trade union cooperation: the revision of the Posting of Workers Directive (PWD) which can be seen in light of the discussion on 'social dumping'. In 2016, the European Commission proposed a revision of the PWD and it led to a great deal of debate, with a clear East–West division in the reactions. The proposal aimed at eliminating certain kinds of social dumping; the goal was that the same work in the same place should get the same pay. Ministers and parliaments in several Central/Eastern European countries raised their voice against the revision. Employers' organizations were generally negative, while the trade union confederations at European level were positive but not uncritical as they wanted a more radical reform. No manifest East–West cleavage became visible in the trade union movement. Even in countries dismissive of the revision, the main labour organizations supported the dominant union responses.

In the concluding Chapter 5, we summarize the results presented in our analyses and revisit some of the contextual and theoretical discussion from the introductory chapter. The purpose of this is to draw some general conclusions regarding the importance of understanding trade union cooperation as dependent on organizational and other power resources and the varieties of industrial relations and sectoral regimes across Europe.

Trade Unions and Industrial Relations in Europe

A *trade union* may be defined as 'a continuous association of wage-earners for the purpose of maintaining or improving the conditions of their employment' (Webb and Webb 1894: 1). By organizing in associations, workers can avoid underbidding each other in the labour market and they can defend or improve joint standards for employment and working conditions, either directly in collective bargaining with the employers or indirectly by influencing state regulations. The establishment of trade unions and collective bargaining institutions can also be beneficial to employer organizations and national governments, since they may help to 'maintain social peace and ensure the legitimacy of managerial control' (Traxler 1998: 208).

The aim and function of unions in the labour market and in society can ideal-typically be depicted as threefold, and the balance between these three aspects varies by tradition across Europe (Hyman 2001b). From a labour market point of view, trade unions (and employer organizations) may be seen as *economic cartels* negotiating the price of work and employment conditions. According to this approach, the organizations mainly defend the interests of their members, who may be employees in a specific company, in certain occupations, or in a specific sector of the economy. From a political point of view, unions may be regarded as *social movements* aimed at resource mobilization for the working class in general to influence state regulations of employment and working conditions or even to address more universal issues concerning wealth and welfare. The solidarity of unions in this approach extends far beyond their members. The third aim and function of trade unions can be said to relate to overall social cohesion. They are then seen as *civil society organizations* bridging the contradiction between labour and capital in 'social partnership', dialogue and compromise (Hyman 2001b: 38–63). This approach is thus less related to antagonistic relations and conflict, but rather to overall 'social responsibilities' of the organizations. Unions are assumed to cooperate with employers and the state for the overall good for workers and companies in a certain sector of the economy or social cohesion at large.

Trade unions may have different power resources linked to these aims and functions (Gumbrell-McCormick and Hyman 2013: 30–35; Lehndorff et al. 2017). Their *organizational power* is based on their number of members, who through membership fees may build up financial and staffing resources. Unions below the confederate level may range from a few hundred or a few thousand members to millions of members, as in the German services union *Ver.di*. This of course affects their possibilities of financing and staffing various operations as well as mobilizing members in action. Still, the most important may not be whether a trade union has a large number of members, but whether or not it organizes a large proportion of the employees. Just to give a sense of such differences we can mention that overall union density in Europe varies from around 4.5% in Estonia to above 90% in Iceland (Visser 2019). Another dimension is s*tructural power* that is close to organizational power, but is more about the bargaining strength of unions versus employers—in their company, occupation, sector or the economy at large. This kind of strength is also a function of unemployment levels and employers' demand for labour. A third component is unions' *institutional power* that has to do with their legal (institutionalized) rights to organize, be consulted, bargain, have their agreements legally extended and take industrial action. Unions' *societal power*, finally, is based on their ability to build alliances with political or civil society organizations and influence public discourse. All these forms of power differ substantially across countries and at the same time it must be stressed that they are not independent of each other.

The concept of *industrial relations* broadly refers to '*/i/nteraction* between employers, employees, and the government; and the *institutions* and *associations* through which such interactions are mediated' (Brown et al. 2018; italics added). The three italicized aspects of industrial relations were already emphasized when the concept was theoretically elaborated for analyses at national level, that is, rules, collective action, bargaining and power relations were in focus (Dunlop 1958). By emphasizing one of them above the others, we may actually talk about three different approaches to industrial relations. A strong focus on the *associations*—trade unions, employer organizations and the government and their collective interests and power resources—leans towards political economy and Marxist conflict-oriented traditions. If instead concentrating on the *relations* and *interactions* between the collective actors—through social dialogue, bargaining, lobbying or contentious action such as demonstration strikes, blockades and lockouts—there is a turn towards more of a strategic action perspective (Hyman 2001a: 5). Lastly, a concentration on the *institutional* aspect of industrial relations—for example the regulative, normative and cultural-cognitive frames in which the collective actors and their interactions are embedded and reproduced (Godard 2004)—tends towards a sociological or organizational neo-institutionalist approach. In this case, there is inspiration from older theories based on functionalist reasoning. As we see it, the differences between these views are not so much an issue of what is fundamental in an ontological sense, since frequently in research all three aspects exist and are mutually interdependent. This can be illustrated by the definition of industrial relations as 'institutional arrangements shaped by legislative frameworks, historical traditions, accumulated vested interests and learned patterns of behaviour' (Hyman 1994: 1).

Even if the concept of industrial relations was originally developed to study the institutionalized interactions between employers and employees within nation states, it is today often used in comparative and even transnational analyses. There are at least three different approaches to such studies and we will now briefly discuss these in turn.

Comparisons of Industrial Relations in Europe

The most direct way to study European industrial relations is to compare national industrial relations across countries. Such an approach commonly focuses on structural factors. The main ones used are trade union and employer membership, the organizations' power resources and the power balance between them, local employee representation, collective bargaining styles and coverage, levels of coordination or centralization of bargaining, the social partners' political influence and the role of the state (e.g., Baccaro and Howell 2017; Visser et al. 2009; Henning 2015).

In dealing with a large number of countries, such comparisons run the risk of getting quite messy. Thus, some selection of a smaller set of countries is often needed in order to produce and present results in digestible form. One possibility is that the selection is made on the basis of a 'varieties-of-capitalism' perspective (Baccaro and Howell 2017; Bamber et al. 2016; Seeliger 2019). Another approach, which is commonly applied in research including European and international comparisons, is to cluster countries on the basis of similarities into a smaller set of *regimes* of industrial relations (Visser et al. 2009; Eurofound 2017) or *varieties* or *models* of trade unionism (Gumbrell-McCormick and Hyman 2013: 6–28; Hyman 2001b; Lehndorff et al. 2017).

Without a doubt these attempts to reduce variation have significant advantages, but they can also have disadvantages, by reducing the existing diversity too much. Anyway, we will try them out to test their explanatory power. We will soon discover their limitations, for example in connection with specific problematic topics in union cooperation, such as the question of statutory minimum wages to be dealt with in Chapter 3.

Empirically grounded typologies of European countries with a smaller set of regimes or models of trade unionism—or welfare regimes, varieties of capitalism, or employment regimes for that matter—generally tend to single out the same geographic clusters of countries. We use the regional terms Central/Eastern Europe, Central/Western Europe, Nordic region, Southern Europe and Western Europe. Some central characteristics of the regimes in these clusters are presented in Table 1.1 and will be elaborated briefly.

Table 1.1 Industrial relations regimes in Europe

	Central/Eastern Europe	Central/Western Europe	Nordic countries	Southern Europe	Western Europe
IR regime	Transitional (fragmented)	Social partnership	Organized corporatism	Polarized/state-centred	Liberal pluralism
Union density	Low to moderate (4–24%)	Moderate (17–53%)	High (51–90%)	Low to moderate (8–34%)	Moderate (23–25%)[a]
Social partner organization	Both sides weak	Both sides strong	Both sides strong	Variable	Both sides strong
Power balance	Employer-oriented	Balanced	Labour-oriented	Alternating	Employer-oriented
Bargaining style	Acquiescent/ uncoordinated	Integrated/ coordinated	Integrated/ coordinated	Conflictual/ uncoordinated	Conflictual/ uncoordinated
Role of the state	Limited/transition oriented	Shadow of hierarchy	Limited/ mediating	Frequent intervention	Non-intervention
Partners' role in public policy	Irregular/politicized	Institutionalized influence	Institutionalized influence	Irregular/politicized	Rare/event-driven

[a]Figures refer to the main Western European countries: the UK and Ireland. Union density for Malta is 52% and for Cyprus 44%

Sources Visser et al. (2009), Visser (2019), cf. Bechter and Brandl (2015a), Gumbrell-McCormick and Hyman (2013)

The many Central/Eastern European countries are quite diverse and it may be questioned whether they make up a regime at all. As we can see in Table 1.1, they are classified as belonging to a *transitional* or *fragmented* regime of industrial relations. The term transitional refers to the changes from the previous state socialist systems to liberal market economies, while 'fragmented' signals both the variation between countries and the social partners' generally low degree of organization and coordination within countries. Trade unions are quite weak in most of these nations, union density is generally low and workers usually do not identify that strongly with unions, partly because of their history. The tradition of contentious action is weak, and several countries have clear restrictions on the right to strike. Bargaining is mostly decentralized to the company level, and even though national confederations exist, in many countries the sectoral level is undeveloped. The social partners have relatively little bargaining autonomy, as governments frequently have been more concerned with the transition to a market economy than with regulating labour relations (e.g., Bieler and Schulten 2008; Henning 2015; Visser et al. 2009).

The Central/Western European countries Austria, Belgium, Germany, Luxembourg, the Netherlands and Switzerland are described as having a social partnership tradition (Bieler and Schulten 2008; Visser et al. 2009). Slovenia was later added to this category. In these countries, there are developed tripartite and corporatist relations between trade unions, employers and the state. They are thus said to belong to a *social partnership regime* of industrial relations. The social partners have a high degree of autonomy from the state, collective bargaining coverage is generally high because of legal extension mechanisms, and unions' political influence is fairly strong. Union density is moderate, although much higher in Belgium (2017: 53%) than in the other countries. The main level of bargaining is sectoral and the levels of industrial conflict are relatively low, among other things because of the cooperative social partnership approach. There is also a tradition of religiously based organizations. Employee representation is typically organized in a dual system including both union representation and work councils.

The Nordic countries—Denmark, Finland, Iceland, Norway and Sweden—are in contrast to Central/Eastern Europe rather homogenous in their industrial relations systems (e.g., Jochem 2011; Visser et al. 2009). Their industrial relations regime is labelled *organized corporatism*, characterized by strong employer organizations and unions negotiating collective agreements with a high degree of autonomy from the state and with high coverage. The national confederations are largely organized on the basis of social class, as opposed to the ideological and religious divisions in some other parts of Europe. The autonomy of bargaining and the strength of unions have created a need for them to take responsibility for the functioning of the labour markets. With the help of state mediation and conflict resolution, the level of open conflict between the partners has been kept relatively low. Despite their autonomy, the Nordic unions have since long comparatively strong influence on government policies, because of their organizational strength and historical connection to social democratic parties and governments. They also have quite well coordinated organizations through their single-channel representation from company to national confederate levels, but with collective bargaining centred at the sectoral level.

In the Southern part of Europe, France, Greece, Italy, Portugal and Spain are said to make up a *polarized/state-centred regime* of industrial relations (Bieler and Schulten 2008; Visser et al. 2009). This regime is based on traditions of conflict between employer organizations and trade unions. It entails a more fragmented union movement divided according to political and religious differences. Other features are relatively weak coordination between different levels of bargaining and rather low union density. There is a variation in the principal level of bargaining between countries and we find both single- and dual-channel representation. Southern European countries show more of politicized involvement of the social partners and more frequent state intervention into the determination of wages and labour standards compared to the Nordic region and Central/Western Europe. Strikes are seen as an important means of political protest to influence the state to take action.

Western European countries—the United Kingdom and Ireland—are categorized as belonging to a *liberal pluralist* regime, to which also Malta and Cyprus are sometimes added (Bieler and Schulten 2008; Visser et al.

2009). This regime is characterized by lower degrees of state intervention in industrial relations and less of legally established standard provisions than the Southern European, Nordic and Central/Eastern European regimes. Unions' involvement in policy-making is more ad hoc in nature. Collective agreement coverage is relatively low, even though union density is moderate compared to European overall levels. Trade union coordination is more fragmented than in the Nordic and Central/Western European regions, which is linked to the fact that collective bargaining is more decentralized, with company bargaining as typical.

Sectoral Comparisons across Europe

As hinted above, regime typologies can be criticized for hiding some variation between the countries clustered together (Gumbrell-McCormick and Hyman 2013: 8–28; Lehndorff et al. 2017). The Nordic regime appears to be the most homogenous, whereas Central/Eastern Europe is a quite heterogeneous region. Another aspect is the variation in industrial relations within each of the countries. There can actually be more diversity in industrial relations across sectors within a country than within sectors in the EU (Bechter et al. 2012). From this point of view, it has been suggested that it is better to compare sectors than regimes. We may even speak about *sectoral regimes* of industrial relations in Europe (Bechter and Brandl 2015b).

The basis for a sectoral approach in the study of industrial relations is that industries differ in many ways—for example, in terms of work organization, production processes and market frameworks. The sectoral (economic) context may thus influence industrial relations more strongly than national (political) contexts (Bechter and Brandl 2015b). If also taking into consideration that labour organizations in different sectors may have diverging identities, resources and relations to employers, it is likely that we can uncover effects on the engagement in European union cooperation. Sector differences can also impact on the more specific balance regarding unions' choices of which channels to work through and of what strategies to pursue in relation to EU policies.

With respect to sectoral differences we should note that some industries, particularly manufacturing, operate on highly integrated product markets with high exposure to international competition. If their work organization enables a high degree of production transferability, the trade unions need to embark on transnational cooperation. More 'sheltered' industries—such as healthcare and education—are less exposed to international competition and have less opportunity for production relocation across borders (Bechter et al. 2012). Trade unions are then under less external pressure to engage in transnational collaboration and have developed it in weaker forms. The opposite applies to unions in sectors under international competitive pressure; they are more likely to be active in cross-border cooperation and lobbying than those in sectors focused more on national markets (Bieler 2005; Gumbrell-McCormick and Hyman 2013: 160).

Some reservations have to be added to this argument. Industries that have undergone liberalization, such as civil aviation and telecommunications, and sectors that in other ways have been heavily affected by EU policies have also had strong motives to collaborate across borders to try to influence these policies (Müller et al. 2010). An example worth mentioning is the construction sector that has been greatly affected by the posting of workers. Moreover, there are significant sectoral differences in terms of union organization and resources. Trade unions in manufacturing usually have a stronger organization and more resources nationally, compared to unions in services and professional occupations.

European-Level Industrial Relations

The third way to approach industrial relations in Europe is to look at the existence of European-level *associations, interactions* and *institutions*, making up a relatively autonomous set-up of industrial relations structures at supranational level (Marginson and Sisson 2004; Smismans 2012). To begin with the *collective actors*, consisting of employee and employer associations and the state, we find a structure similar to that at national level, with tripartite relations between these actors. There are also supranational relations between employers and workers in cross-sectoral, sectoral and company-level organs. The European Commission, the European Council and other EU institutions then make up the actors taking the role of the state in the European setting. Social partner organizations exist at both cross-industry and sectoral levels. On the labour side, the main actor is the cross-industry ETUC and its sister organization *Eurocadres*, which is a joint European association for professionals and managers in both the private and the public sector. The ETUC was established in 1973 from already existing trade union cooperation in the EEC and EFTA countries, aimed at both lobbying and getting access to decision-making structures (Dølvik 1997: 134–150; cf. Degryse and Tilly 2013). There are approximately 90 peak-level confederations as members of the ETUC and, additionally, ten sector-based European Trade Union Federations (ETUFs). Eurocadres was founded in 1993 and has about 60 national trade unions and six of the ETUFs as member organizations. The counterparts at cross-industry level are the employer organizations BusinessEurope (previously called UNICE) with roughly 40 national business federations as affiliates, CEEP representing public sector employers, and SMEunited (previously called UEAPME) with circa 70 national organizations representing small- and medium-sized employers.

Moving on to the *institutions* and *interactions*, we find arenas for bipartite negotiations and access points to EU policy-making for both employer organizations and trade unions. These have been developed over a long time and to some extent they mirror at least a minimal set of industrial relations institutions at national level (Rhodes 2015). The European-level social partners have a number of access points to EU policy-making by being invited to *consultations* in various committees, for example the Economic and Social Committee, the Standing Committee on Employment, the Macroeconomic Dialogue, and the European Semester. However, unions have quite limited power in these, which have been said to be channels more for information and advice than for influencing policy development (Welz 2008: 217–278).

There are also institutionalized arenas for bipartite dialogue between employers and trade unions through the *Social Dialogue* at cross-industry as well as sectoral levels. The European Social Dialogue (ESD) was brought about in the mid-1980s to facilitate collective bargaining and regulation at cross-industry level between the ETUC, on the one hand, and BusinessEurope, CEEP and SMEunited, on the other. The idea was that the social partners should be given possibilities to contribute to European integration and to a strengthening of the EU's social dimension (Tricart 2019). With the institutionalization of the ESD in 1987, the social partners acquired the right of forming binding agreements that could be converted into directives and they thus obtained a function as a corporatist, semi-legislative organ (Welz 2008). During its first decade, the ESD at cross-industry level produced a few agreements that were turned into directives, but not without pressure from the European Commission (Welz 2008: 381–385). A second avenue was also instituted through the right to produce autonomous bipartite agreements to be implemented by the partners themselves rather than through directives. In the late 1990s, with the European Commission taking a step back, the ESD became mainly bipartite and autonomous and its regulatory effect decreased (Welz 2008: 258–340; Rhodes 2015; Prosser 2016).

Table 1.2 gives some examples in which the social partners had an indirect consultative role or direct involvement in producing important regulations—and in the case of autonomous agreements also in implementing them. The information in the table both provides further information on the regulative pillars of European-level institutions and illustrates some important interaction outcomes from these institutions.

Sectoral European-Level Industrial Relations

Just as at national level, we also have European trade union and employer organizations at sectoral level. On its webpage concerning social dialogue, the European Commission lists 15 sectoral ETUFs.[1] Like the ETUC, the ETUFs—previously called European Industry Federations (EIFs)—are *meta-organizations*, that is, they have organizations as members (Ahrne and Brunsson 2008). The ETUF members are trade unions below the peak level, organized from broad sectoral bases. Some of the main ones are listed below:

1 Why and How to Study Trade Union Cooperation in Europe?

- European Federation of Building and Woodworkers (EFBWW)
- European Federation of Food, Agriculture and Tourism trade Unions (EFFAT)
- European Federation of Public Service Unions (EPSU)
- European Trade Union Committee for Education (ETUCE)
- European Transport Workers' Federation (ETF)
- European Trade Union Federation for Services and Communication (UNI-Europa)
- IndustriALL Europe[2]

Table 1.2 Directives and agreements of cross-industry relevance

A) Directives from the ordinary legislative procedure
European Works Councils, 1994 (rev. 2009): Rules for EWCs in companies operating in at least two European Economic Area countries
Posting of workers (PWD), 1996 (rev. 2018): Regulates remuneration for posted workers, long-term posting and more
Working time, 2003: Regulates weekly working time, rest and leave, with a maximum of 48 hours average weekly working time
Services, 2006: Facilitates trade in services between countries. Several sectors exempt
Temporary Agency Work, 2008: Provides workers from employment agencies similar conditions as regular employees
Enforcement of PWD, 2014: Aims at a better application of the PWD
B) Negotiated law (Directives from the ESD)
Parental leave, 1995 (rev. 2009): Gives parents the right to 4 months of leave, of which 1 is non-transferable between parents
Part-time work, 1997: Prohibits discrimination of part-time workers
Fixed-term work, 1999: Prohibits discrimination of temporary employees
C) Autonomous agreements (from the ESD)
Telework, 2002: Regulates teleworkers conditions, health and safety and collective rights
Work-related stress, 2004: Prescribes measures to prevent and manage work-related stress
Harassment and violence, 2007: Prescribes measures to prevent and deal with bullying, sexual harassment and violence
Inclusive labour markets, 2010: Prescribes measures for marginalized and disadvantaged groups in the labour market
Active ageing, 2010: Aims to create good conditions for workers of all ages

Sources European Commission webpage and Social Dialogue texts database

In addition to these, there are also some sector-narrower ETUFs. The employer side at sectoral level is more fragmented and the European Commission lists more than 60 such meta-organizations. However, these include both cross-national employer associations and organizations that are more of business associations with national members based on industry interest rather than on a status as employers.

Already before the ESD was instituted, some sectors had voluntary social dialogues between the social partners at European level. In 1998, the European Commission wanted to supplement the cross-industry ESD and therefore reorganized the informal sectoral committees into formally recognized and co-funded European Sectoral Social Dialogue (ESSD) committees. These were provided with similar opportunities of producing negotiated law and bipartite agreements as the cross-industry ESD had been given in the 1980s (Degryse 2015; Keller and Weber 2011). Since their establishment, the number of ESSD committees has expanded from around 20 to well over 40. They cover different sectors and from their formation to the present, they have produced over 900 documents co-signed by employers and unions. Yet, only very few of these outcomes are autonomous agreements or negotiated law (Table 1.3). The majority are lobbying statements, procedural documents and soft instruments such as declarations, tools and recommendations that have quite little effect at national level. Some of the last attempts at producing negotiated law from the ESSDs have actually been blocked politically, for example the agreements on health and safety in hairdressing and on information and consultation rights for government employees (Tricart 2019).

Table 1.3 Directives and agreements of sectoral relevance

A) Negotiated law (Directives and [blocked Directives] from ESSD)
Working time of seafarers, 1999
Working time in civil aviation, 2000
Working conditions in railway cross-border services, 2004
Health and security on ships, 2008
Prevention from sharp injuries in hospitals and healthcare, 2009
[Health and safety in hairdressing, Agreement 2012/2016; no directive]
Working time in inland waterway transport, 2014
[Information and consultations rights in central government administrations, Agreement 2015; no directive]
Working conditions in fishing, 2016
B) Autonomous agreements (from ESSD)
European license for (train) drivers, 2004
Health protection—good handling and use of crystalline silica, 2006
European hairdressing certificates, 2009
Minimum requirements for contracts in professional football, 2012

Sources European Commission webpage and Social Dialogue texts database

Data Collection Methods and Empirical Materials

Empirically, this book is based on data collected during two major research projects performed in the period 2009–2019. The first project, *Can Trade Unions within Europe Cooperate?*, was headed by Bengt Furåker and was funded by the Swedish Council for Working Life and Social Research (FAS 2008-0246). The second project, called *Conditions for and Obstacles to Trade Union Cooperation in Europe. A Comparative Study of Countries and Sectors*, was led by Bengt Larsson and received funding from Riksbankens Jubileumsfond (RJ P13-0776:1). Besides ourselves, our research team included Mattias Bengtsson, Kristina Lovén Seldén, Patrik Vulkan and Anton Törnberg.

The data collected in these projects cover two surveys, a total of 46 interviews with 55 trade union officials from different countries, documents of various kinds and data from existing databases. It should also be mentioned that one of the members of our research team was allowed to participate in the ETUC Executive Committee's meetings during a period and could thus make direct observations. We begin by presenting the surveys and the interviews and end by saying a few words about the documents and databases used.

Quantitative Materials

In both surveys, the aim was to study trade union positions, activities and strategies, that is, the focus was on the organizational and not the individual level. Since we only requested one questionnaire per union, we targeted top-level representatives who could legitimately respond for the whole organization. A majority of the respondents were secretaries-general, presidents or vice presidents, and the rest of the respondents had positions like international secretaries or other high-level officials. The surveys were translated into several languages, and we used a mixed-mode approach to improve the response rates. The first two waves of send-outs were web-based and a third wave was postal (Fan and Yan 2010).

Survey 1 was distributed in 2010–2011 to all member organizations of the ETUC—that is, the 85 national confederations and the 12 EIFs (ETUFs) which were ETUC members at the time of the investigation. Moreover, we included 499 trade unions below the peak level in 14 European countries (Austria, Belgium, Denmark, Finland, France, Germany, Iceland, Ireland, Norway, Poland, Spain, Sweden, Switzerland and the United Kingdom). The selection of unions in these countries was grounded on an ambition to target unions with approximately 10,000 members or more. The total response rate was 42% (Table 1.4), but if

Table 1.4 Information on survey 1 by region, 2010–2011

Region	Number of answers (response rates)	Number of unions in send-out
Central/Eastern Europe	31 (20%)	157
Central/Western Europe	46 (49%)	93
Nordic region	102 (70%)	146
Southern Europe	35 (26%)	137
Western Europe[a]	27 (53%)	51
EIFs/ETUFs	9 (75%)	12
Total	250 (42%)	596

[a]Including Cyprus and Malta (for details, see Larsson 2012)

not counting France and Poland in which we had difficulties in selecting unions with at least 10,000 members—because of the fragmented system with a large number of small unions—the response rate was over 70%. Besides some background matters regarding the size of union and who was responding, survey 1 contained general questions about union cooperation and two sets of questions specifically about wage and working time issues.

Survey 2 was distributed in 2015–2016 to 602 trade unions in 36 European countries. We directed it to unions in six main sectors according to an established typology (Crouch 1999): mining (extractive), metal, construction (productive/transformative), transport (distributive), healthcare, and banking and finance (public and private services). This strategic selection was designed to achieve large variation in aspects identified as important for sectoral union cooperation: production processes, work organization, possibilities for relocation and exposure to international competition. The overall response rate was 37%, with a total of 221 answers (Table 1.5). The sectors of mining and metals are merged in our analyses, because many unions organized employees in both sectors. Furthermore, an extra category of multisectoral unions was created to gather unions organizing employees in more than one of the sectors. In addition to asking about size and sector and who the respondent was, survey 2 enclosed wide-ranging questions about union cooperation and a set of questions specifically about wage issues.

Given the response rates on both surveys, a general note of caution as regards the results is required. From our attempts to recruit interviewees

Table 1.5 Information on survey 2 by region, 2015–2016

Region	Number of answers (response rates)	Number of unions in send-out
Central/Eastern Europe	69 (27%)	255
Central/Western Europe	35 (39%)	89
Nordic region	73 (62%)	117
Southern Europe	35 (32%)	110
Western Europe[a]	9 (18%)	51
Total	221 (37%)	602

[a]Including Cyprus and Malta (for details, see Larsson [2012] and Vulkan and Larsson [2019], online supplementary material)

(see below), we got the impression that the lesser the trade unions participated in transnational cooperation, the less inclined they were to take part in this research. Thus, both the survey and the interviews may be biased in the sense that the level of cross-border collaboration shown is higher than it is among the non-responding unions. Another problem is the large differences in response rates across regions.

Qualitative Materials

In total, we conducted 46 interviews with 55 top-level or senior officials in the two projects. The interviews were semi-structured and lasted around 1–2 hours. They were done in person, via Skype or telephone and in one case via e-mail. The conversations were recorded and transcribed verbatim—except for two for which only a summary was written, because the respondents did not want to be recorded or quoted directly. We coded the interviews thematically using software for qualitative analysis.

The first interview study included 17 interviews conducted in 2011–2012 in connection with the first survey. These had a thematic orientation on wage issues, with some focus on minimum wages. Respondents were chosen to represent different national views on the main topics: Belgium (3 interviews), Germany (5), Latvia (1), Spain (3) and Sweden (5). Ten of the interviewees represented cross-sectoral confederations and seven represented sectoral or multisectoral trade unions (cf. Furåker and Lovén Seldén 2013: 510–511).

The second interview study was done during 2015–2016, close to the second survey. We conducted 29 interviews, with unions in healthcare (8), construction (5), metal (5), banking and finance (5), and transport (3). From recommendations by contacts in Central/Eastern Europe, we also included one union confederation and one union each in education and energy in that region. Our selection aimed to achieve a variation in sectors and regions corresponding to the survey. The Nordic countries were represented by Sweden (7) and a joint Nordic labour organization (1); Central/Western Europe by Germany (4); Southern Europe by Italy (5); Central/Eastern Europe by the Czech Republic (3), Hungary (3),

Latvia (2) and Lithuania (1); and Western Europe by the United Kingdom (3) (cf. Larsson and Törnberg 2019: 7).

Besides the interviews, we also utilized documents and data from other sources: We made use of European Commission documents, webpages and the Social Dialogue Texts Database to get information on social dialogues and their outcomes. Another source of information was the ICTWSS Database on Institutional Characteristics of Trade Unions, Wage Setting, State Intervention and Social Pacts in 55 countries between 1960 and 2017 (Visser 2019). We were also given access to certain data from the ETUC, of which we primarily used the minutes of the ETUC Executive Committee meetings (Furåker and Lovén Seldén 2016). It should be repeated that one member of the research team had the possibility of attending some of these meetings.

Notes

1. https://ec.europa.eu/social/main.jsp?catId=329&langId=en (accessed October 8, 2019).
2. IndustriALL was established through a 2012 merger of the European Metalworkers' Federation (EMF), the European Mine, Chemical and Energy Workers Federation (EMCEF) and the European Trade Union Committee: Textile, Clothing and Leather (ETUC-TCL).

References

Ahrne, G., and N. Brunsson. 2008. *Meta-organizations*. Cheltenham: Edward Elgar.

Baccaro, L., and C. Howell. 2017. *Trajectories of Neoliberal Transformation: European Industrial Relations Since the 1970s*. Cambridge: Cambridge University Press.

Bamber, G.J., R.D. Lansbury, N. Wailes, and C.F. Wright (eds.). 2016. *International and Comparative Employment Relations*, 6th ed. London: Sage.

Bechter, B., and B. Brandl. 2015a. Developments in European Industrial Relations. In *Industrial Relations in Europe 2014*, 17–40. Brussels: European Commission.

Bechter, B., and B. Brandl. 2015b. Measurement and Analysis of Industrial Relations Aggregates: What Is the Relevant Unit of Analysis in Comparative Research? *European Political Science* 14 (4): 422–438.

Bechter, B., B. Brandl, and G. Meardi. 2012. Sectors or Countries? Typologies and Levels of Analysis in Comparative Industrial Relations. *European Journal of Industrial Relations* 18 (3): 185–202.

Bieler, A. 2005. European Integration and the Transnational Restructuring of Social Relations: The Emergence of Labour as a Regional Actor? *Journal of Common Market Studies* 43 (3): 461–484.

Bieler, A., and T. Schulten. 2008. European Integration: A Strategic Level for Trade Union Resistance to Neoliberal Restructuring and for the Promotion of Political Alternatives? In *Labour and the Challenges of Globalization—What Prospects for Transnational Solidarity?* ed. A. Bieler, I. Lindberg, and D. Pillay, 231–247. London: Pluto Press.

Brown, G.W., I. McLean, and A. McMillan. 2018. Industrial Relations. In *A Concise Oxford Dictionary of Politics and International Relations*. Oxford: Oxford University Press.

Bücker, A., and W. Warneck (eds.). 2010. *Viking—Laval—Rüffert: Consequences and Policy Perspectives*. Brussels: ETUI.

Crouch, C. 1999. *Social Change in Western Europe*. Oxford: Oxford University Press.

Degryse, C. 2015. *The European Sectoral Social Dialogue: An Uneven Record of Achievement?*. Brussels: ETUI.

Degryse, C., and P. Tilly. 2013. *1973–2013: 40 Years of History of the European Trade Union Confederation*. Brussels: ETUI.

Dølvik, J.E. 1997. *Redrawing Boundaries of Solidarity? ETUC, Social Dialogue and the Europeanization of Trade Unions in the 1990s*. Oslo: Fafo.

Dunlop, J.T. 1958. *Industrial Relations Systems*. New York: Holt.

Erne, R. 2008. *European Unions: Labor's Quest for a Transnational Democracy*. Ithaca: Cornell University Press.

Eurofound. 2017. *Mapping Varieties of Industrial Relations: Eurofound's Analytical Framework Applied*. Luxembourg: Publications Office of the European Union.

European Commission. 2016. *A New Start for Social Dialogue*. Luxembourg: Publications Office of the European Union.

European Commission. 2017. *European Pillar of Social Rights*. Luxembourg: Publications Office of the European Union.
Fan, W., and Z. Yan. 2010. Factors Affecting Response Rates of the Web Survey: A Systematic Review. *Computers in Human Behavior* 26 (2): 132–139.
Furåker, B., and K. Lovén Seldén. 2013. Trade Union Cooperation on Statutory Minimum Wages? A Study of European Trade Union Positions. *Transfer: European Review of Labour and Research* 19 (4): 507–520.
Furåker, B., and K. Lovén Seldén. 2016. Patterns of Speech Activity at ETUC Executive Committee Meetings, 2005–2012. *European Journal of Industrial Relations* 22 (1): 57–71.
Gajewska, K. 2009. *Transnational Labour Solidarity: Mechanisms of Commitment to Cooperation within the European Trade Union Movement*. London: Routledge.
Godard, J. 2004. The New Institutionalism, Capitalist Diversity, and Industrial Relations. In *Theoretical Perspectives on Work and the Employment Relationship*, ed. B.E. Kaufman, 229–264. Champaign, IL: Industrial Relations Research Association.
Gumbrell-McCormick, R., and R. Hyman. 2013. *Trade Unions in Western Europe: Hard Times, Hard Choices*. Oxford: Oxford University Press.
Hann, D., M. Hauptmeier, and J. Waddington. 2017. European Works Councils After Two Decades. *European Journal of Industrial Relations* 23 (3): 209–224.
Henning, K. 2015. Trade Unions and Industrial Relations in the EU Member States of Eastern Enlargement. In *Interest Representation and Europeanization of Trade Unions from EU Member States of the Eastern Enlargement*, ed. C. Landgraf and H. Pleines, 53–71. Stuttgart: Ibidem.
Hyman, R. 1994. Industrial Relations in Western Europe: An Era of Ambiguity? *Industrial Relations* 33 (1): 1–24.
Hyman, R. 2001a. Trade Union Research and Cross-National Comparison. *European Journal of Industrial Relations* 7 (2): 203–232.
Hyman, R. 2001b. *Understanding European Trade Unionism: Between Market, Class and Society*. London: Sage.
Jochem, S. 2011. Nordic Employment Policies—Change and Continuity before and during the Financial Crisis. *Social Policy & Administration* 45 (11): 131–145.
Keller, B., and S. Weber. 2011. Sectoral Social Dialogue at EU Level: Problems and Prospects of Implementation. *European Journal of Industrial Relations* 17 (3): 227–243.

Kelly, J. 2015. Trade Union Membership and Power in Comparative Perspective. *The Economic and Labour Relations Review* 26 (4): 526–544.
Larsson, B. 2012. Obstacles to Transnational Trade Union Cooperation in Europe—Results from a European Survey. *Industrial Relations Journal* 43 (2): 152–170.
Larsson, B., and A. Törnberg. 2019. Sectoral Networks of Transnational Trade Union Cooperation in Europe. *Economic and Industrial Democracy*. Published online ahead of print. https://doi.org/10.1177/0143831x19853871.
Lehndorff, S., H. Dribbusch, and T. Schulten. 2017. European Trade Unions in a Time of Crises—An Overview. In *Rough Waters: European Trade Unions in a Time of Crises*, ed. S. Lehndorff, H. Dribbusch, and T. Schulten, 7–35. ETUI: Brussels.
Marginson, P. 2015. Coordinated Bargaining in Europe: From Incremental Corrosion to Frontal Assault? *European Journal of Industrial Relations* 21 (2): 97–114.
Marginson, P., and K. Sisson. 2004. *European Integration and Industrial Relations: Multi-Level Governance in the Making*. Basingstoke: Palgrave Macmillan.
Müller, T., H.-W. Platzer, and S. Rüb. 2010. Transnational Company Policy and Coordination of Collective Bargaining—New Challenges and Roles for European Industry Federations. *Transfer: European Review of Labour and Research* 16 (4): 509–524.
Perin, E., and E. Léonard. 2011. European Sectoral Social Dialogue and National Social Partners. *Transfer: European Review of Labour and Research* 17 (2): 159–168.
Prosser, T. 2016. Economic Union without Social Union: The Strange Case of the European Social Dialogue. *Journal of European Social Policy* 26 (5): 460–472.
Rhodes, M. 2015. Employment Policy: Between Efficacy and Experimentation. In *Policy Making in the European Union*, ed. H. Wallace, M.A. Pollack, and A.R. Young, 294–317. Oxford: Oxford University Press.
Scharpf, F.W. 1996. Negative and Positive Integration in the Political Economy of European Welfare States. In *Governance in the European Union*, ed. G. Marks, F.W. Scharpf, P.C. Schmitter, and W. Streeck, 15–39. London: Sage.
Seeliger, M. 2019. *Trade Unions in the Course of European Integration: The Social Construction of Organized Interests*. London: Routledge.
Smismans, S. (ed.). 2012. *The European Union and Industrial Relations: New Procedures, New Contexts*. Manchester: Manchester University Press.

Traxler, F. 1998. Collective Bargaining in the OECD: Developments, Preconditions and Effects. *European Journal of Industrial Relations* 4 (2): 207–226.

Tricart, J.P. 2019. *Legislative Implementation of European Social Partner Agreements: Challenges and Debates*. Brussels: ETUI.

Visser, J. 2019. ICTWSS Database. Version 6.0. Amsterdam: Amsterdam Institute for Advanced Labour Studies (AIAS), University of Amsterdam.

Visser, J., M. Beentjes, M. van Gerven, and V. Di Stasio. 2009. The Quality of Industrial Relations and the Lisbon Strategy. In *Industrial Relations in Europe 2008*, 45–72. Luxembourg: Publications Office of the European Union.

Vulkan, P., and B. Larsson. 2019. Patterns of Transnational Trade Union Cooperation in Europe: The Effects of Regimes, Sectors and Resources. *European Journal of Industrial Relations* 25 (2): 147–162.

Webb, S., and B. Webb. 1894. *The History of Trade Unionism*. London: Longmans, Green, and Co.

Welz, C. 2008. *The European Social Dialogue Under Articles 138 and 139 of the EC Treaty: Actors, Processes, Outcomes*. Alphen aan den Rijn: Kluwer.

Whittall, M., H. Knudsen, and F. Huijgen (eds.). 2007. *Towards a European Labour Identity: The Case of the European Works Council*. London: Routledge.

Open Access This chapter is licensed under the terms of the Creative Commons Attribution 4.0 International License (http://creativecommons.org/licenses/by/4.0/), which permits use, sharing, adaptation, distribution and reproduction in any medium or format, as long as you give appropriate credit to the original author(s) and the source, provide a link to the Creative Commons license and indicate if changes were made.

The images or other third party material in this chapter are included in the chapter's Creative Commons license, unless indicated otherwise in a credit line to the material. If material is not included in the chapter's Creative Commons license and your intended use is not permitted by statutory regulation or exceeds the permitted use, you will need to obtain permission directly from the copyright holder.

2

Patterns of Transnational Trade Union Cooperation in Europe

Abstract This chapter offers an overview of patterns of transnational trade union cooperation—based on empirical data. It begins by providing a brief depiction of the multilevel structures of such cooperation, followed by a presentation of the general views among unions regarding the importance and the potential benefits of cooperating at different levels. A second section entails a more detailed investigation of the importance attributed to various topics to collaborate on. This part also includes an examination of the preferences among unions in different sectors and industrial relations regimes/regions regarding forms of cooperation. The remainder of the chapter section scrutinizes what unions consider to be the most important obstacles to and facilitators for cross-border cooperation.

Keywords Transnational trade union cooperation · Europe · Topics · Obstacles · Facilitators

Introduction

The existence of meta-organizations like the ETUC and the ETUFs, treated in Chapter 1, obviously implies a great deal of cooperation between trade unions in Europe. Even though labour organizations are generally based on national affiliation, we see a long history of internationalism in the trade union movement through both supranational organizations and bilateral contacts and actions (Gumbrell-McCormick and Hyman 2013: 158–161; cf. Gajewska 2009; Seeliger 2019: 14–22). An illustration of how transnational cooperation is highlighted as a joint effort at European level comes from the ETUC action program 2019–2023:

> In recent years we—the ETUC and its affiliates—have significantly strengthened our internal cooperation and coordination. We have agreed on common policies by overcoming the existing differences between east and west, north and south. We have created efficient networks and practices within the ETUC to involve and mobilise our affiliates. We have significantly increased our influence on institutions, at both EU and national level. (ETUC 2019: 8)

Naturally, the level of international activities among the national members of the ETUC and the ETUFs or between trade unions below these peak-level confederations varies across countries and sectors as well as with organizational resources. Some large organizations are active not only in exchange with and support to sister organizations in other countries but are also central drivers and actors on different topics. However, even unions with very small resources and less international activity may actually have strong latent networks of contacts, which can be used when needed—as demonstrated by this quotation from a Baltic interviewee:

> [With some] countries, our cooperation is only a few e-mails [from] time to time, when there is a need… We have more or less at least one person in every country [to whom] we can write or phone to ask some questions. But, the reality is that, like every trade union, we are very busy at the national level, so there are not a lot of international questions we are involved in.

In our two surveys to trade unions, a majority confirmed the general importance of pursuing transnational union cooperation. In survey 1, almost all responding unions (94%) agreed with a statement that cross-national union cooperation will, in the long run, improve conditions for European workers (Larsson 2014). In survey 2, the financial and economic crisis starting in 2008 was said to have had negative effects on transnational cooperation. Over 60% stated that the crisis had made the outlooks of unions more protectionist, thereby substantiating discussions pointing to a 'renationalization' of attitudes during the last decade or so (Lehndorff et al. 2017: 30). Despite this, 70% of the responding unions reported that they had actually increased cooperation with other unions in Europe because of the crisis. In addition, over 40% of the respondents declared that their organization desired even more transnational cooperation in the future (Bengtsson and Vulkan 2018).

In order to unpack such overall ambitions to cooperate for the purpose of improving the conditions for European workers, we need to examine what cooperation between unions really is and what conditions that hinder or facilitate it. In the next section, we begin by introducing a theoretical typology of different collaborative structures and then look at the existing levels of collaboration and how important these are according to the trade unions themselves. Thereafter we focus on the general topics that unions cooperate on and which forms the organizations prefer. The final part of the chapter elaborates the issue of what factors make up important obstacles and facilitators for cooperation.

Multilevel Structures of Cooperation

Theoretically, it is possible to distinguish at least four kinds of cooperative structures signifying different degrees of institutionalization (cf. Müller and Platzer 2017: 294; Müller et al. 2010). (1) The least institutionalized structure consists of bi- or multilateral *communication networks*. Through such networks, national unions can use information from other unions in developing their national or European-level strategies, while still acting independently of others. (2) At the next level, national organizations work jointly to identify common interests and form loose *coordination networks*. This enables them to synchronize their individual actions across countries or at supranational level, for example by matching national collective bargaining or positions to be taken in the ESD, while even then acting autonomously. (3) A still stronger degree of institutionalization is the development of joint activities on a case-by-case basis in *cooperation networks*. Examples of such cooperation can be activities like seminars, training or demonstrations, comprising unions from more than one country. (4) The most institutionalized cooperative structure exists when trade unions together form supranational and staffed *meta-organizations*, that is, with other organizations as members and with a decision-making assembly or a mandate to act on behalf of its affiliates or concert their actions on a more long-term basis (Ahrne and Brunsson 2008). The ETUC and the ETUFs are the main examples at European level.

All of these forms of cooperation exist in Europe and they are only separable analytically. In practice, they are intertwined, since 'joint efforts to build formalized supranational structures for coordination contribute to creating corresponding informal structures (e.g., trust) as a by-product' (Traxler and Mermet 2003: 237). As a consequence, bi- or multilateral communication networks and concerted collaboration through the ETUC and the ETUFs mutually reinforce each other. In that way, top-down and bottom-up processes of cooperation and coordination blend in a multilevel structure (Marginson and Sisson 2004; Keune and Marginson 2013). According to this line of argument, the more concertation there is of action, the stronger the networks of bilateral exchange and informal coordination from below tend to become.

Transnational trade union cooperation simultaneously takes place at various organizational levels and in various regional contexts. From our interviews, we see that unions are active at different levels, from the local to the global. Whereas in small organizations the same individuals may have to be implicated in almost everything, in larger unions there can be an internal division of labour. However, in the practical work around specific topics, the different levels tend to be interwoven also in larger organizations, as shown in this quote from a Swedish union representative:

2 Patterns of Transnational Trade Union Cooperation in Europe

> For us, it is not like 'now we work on European issues' or 'now we work on global issues'... There are several arenas: there is a local, a regional, a national, and there is a European and a global arena. We should be present everywhere—they are all entangled.

By creating a generalized map of a single Swedish trade union's relations to other organizations—both directly to other counterparts and to meta-organizations—it is possible to illustrate the complexity of the multilevel structure of cooperation (Fig. 2.1). The actually existing structures of course vary between countries, sectors and individual unions; the rationale for departing from a Swedish union is that we want to include regional cross-country organizations in the map and those are well developed in the Nordic region.

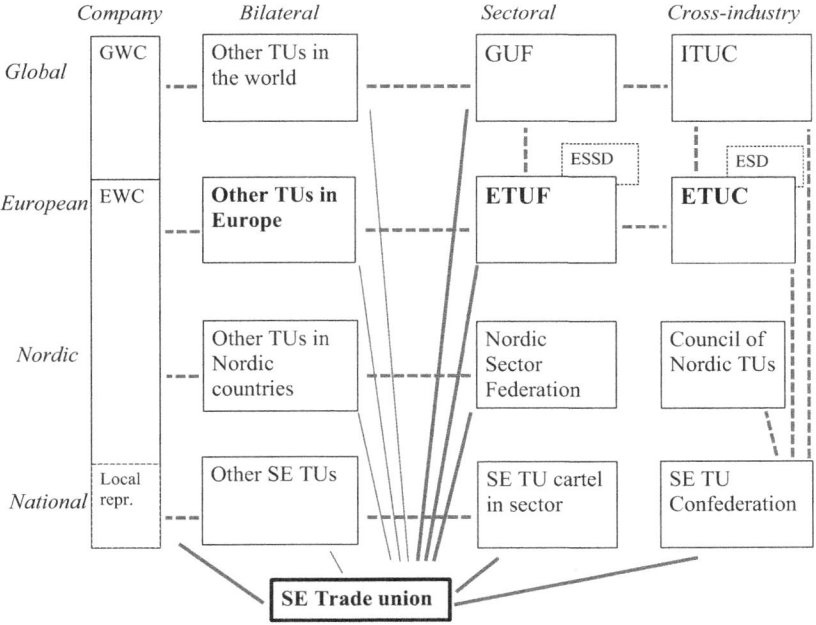

Fig. 2.1 Generalized map of a trade union cooperation structure.
Note GUF = Global Union Federation; GWC = Global Works Council; ITUC = International Trade Union Confederation; SE = Sweden; TU = trade union

Figure 2.1 should be read as follows: The individual union that is the starting point for the structure is placed at the bottom. Thin lines indicate direct bilateral cooperation with other unions within or outside its sector, in- or outside its own country. They refer to everything from more sporadic information exchange or joint action to regular training or support activities. Bold lines signify that the union have representatives in and/or is a member of another organization. Bold dashed lines illustrate similar relationships between these other organizations.

Presented from the left to the right, the structure in Fig. 2.1 demonstrates that, at *company level*, the focal trade union may be involved in local representation and cooperation with other national unions represented in the workplace. Similar cooperation at European and global level can also exist in the form of EWCs in multinational companies having employees in at least two European countries. This may include collaborating in connection with information and consultation processes, contract negotiations with employers and even joint strikes (Banyuls et al. 2008; Müller et al. 2013). A corresponding global-level structure is still very uncommon, although there are some global corporate boards such as Global Works Councils and other similar arrangements (Steiert 2009). The *bilateral level* refers to direct cooperation with other unions within or outside the country and it is usually less formally organized. At *sectoral level*, there may be joint organizations at national level—in Sweden often in the form of union bargaining cartels. In the Nordic region, there are also sectoral Nordic trade union federations. To some extent, these mirror the European-level ETUFs, which have a coordinating role in the 43 ESSD committees. The ETUFs are normally linked to Global Sectoral Federations (GUFs), in some cases as independent subdivisions of the latter. Finally, at *cross-industry level*, there are both national, Nordic, European and global confederations. It can be mentioned that the three national peak-level confederations in Sweden are members of the Council of Nordic Trade Unions, the ETUC and its global counterpart International Trade Union Confederation (ITUC).

The focus of this study is primarily the collaboration at European level in and between the organizations that are in bold in Fig. 2.1. However, from time to time relationships outside of this structure enter as important in the analysis, which is why they are presented in this overview.

We now first examine union views on cooperation within their European meta-organizations (the ETUC and the ETUFs) and then turn to the communication and coordination networks built upon direct bi- and multilateral contacts between national trade unions.

Cooperation within Meta-organizations

Meta-organizations are said to have particular difficulties, because they have other organizations as members (Ahrne and Brunsson 2008; Gumbrell-McCormick and Hyman 2013: 158–161). One of the main tensions and balance acts is that between meta-organizational authority and members' autonomy—in relation to the question of shared identity. In the case of the ETUC, it appears that these issues have been persistent. Nordic and Western European member organizations emphasize autonomy to a greater extent and show doubts to give the ETUC a strong mandate than do Southern and Central/Western European trade unions. This is based on the national traditions of the former, but also on their greater Euroscepticism and reluctance to develop supranational wage policies and regulations (Busemeyer et al., 2008; Dølvik 1997: 162–171, 243–289, 308–309, 392–394; Glassner and Vandaele 2012). Another tension is that between adhering to the 'logic of influence' and leaning towards the 'logic of membership'. It is a matter of the strategic readiness to adjust to the institutional set-up of the EU to become influential as opposed to the attraction to rely on bottom-up democracy and legitimacy, that is, what members perceive as important (Hyman 2005; Erne 2008).

When asked about these issues in survey 1, around 80% of the organizations agreed (to some or a high degree) with the need for the ETUC both to increase efforts to mobilize and pursue the interests of its member organizations and to adapt its methods to the actual decision-making in the EU (Larsson 2014). In other words, this can be interpreted as an appreciation of both the bottom-up logic of membership and the top-down logic of influence. As disclosed in a national-level study, Swedish trade union members had lower expectations on European union cooperation to improve the situation for workers than did the organizations' top-level representatives (Furåker and Bengtsson 2013). Whereas very few of the latter saw any reasons to engage less in issues at European level, 40–50% of their members believed it would be a good idea to do so and instead increase direct efforts to improve working conditions nationally. The tension between a logic of influence and a logic of membership thereby does not merely relate to how the ETUC should function, but also to whether unions should put a lot of effort into such transnational work at all.

As regards meta-organizational authority versus member organizations' autonomy, our survey confirmed continuity in the above variations between different regions/industrial relations regimes in Europe. We pushed the issues to their edge by asking respondents to react to the statement 'To increase their power and influence, the ETUC member organizations must be prepared to transfer authority to the ETUC'. The results in Table 2.1 reveal that besides the ETUFs, trade unions in Central/Eastern Europe more than others believed in such a strategy to enhance influence, whereas the unions in Western European countries and the Nordic region were the ones most strongly underlining autonomy for members' unions. The first column of figures is a summary indicator, showing in what direction unions in each regime/region lean. It is simply the sum of the numbers in columns A and B minus the corresponding sum for columns C and D.

The ETUC is only one meta-organization at European level, and there has been much effort put into the cooperation through the sectoral ETUFs and the ESSDs since around the turn of the millennium. Therefore, in survey 2, we asked representatives for unions at sectoral level about the importance of collaboration through meta-organizations (from national confederations to global confederations). Table 2.2 presents the outcomes on whether it had become more or less important for the responding union in the past ten years to cooperate through different types of organizations. The balance score indicates the extent to which the importance of a specific meta-organization has increased or decreased.

There was a general tendency that trade union meta-organizations, federations and confederations at both national and supranational level were perceived to have become more important for union cooperation

2 Patterns of Transnational Trade Union Cooperation in Europe

Table 2.1 Trade unions' readiness to transfer authority to the ETUC. Percentages ($n = 246$)

	Summary indicator[b]	To a high degree	To some degree	To a low degree	Not at all	Do not know	Total (n)
Central/Western Europe	**14**	6	50	29	13	2	100 (45)
Central/Eastern Europe	**39**	19	49	16	13	3	100 (31)
Nordic region	**−44**	2	24	36	34	4	100 (101)
Southern Europe	**2**	14	37	43	6	0	100 (35)
Western Europe[a]	**−48**	–	24	36	36	2	100 (25)
ETUFs	**10**	22	33	45	0	0	100 (9)

[a]Including Cyprus and Malta
[b]Summary indicator = (To a high degree + To some degree) − (To a low degree + Not at all)
Source Own data, survey 1

Table 2.2 Perceived importance of meta-organizations for trade union cooperation in the last 10 years. Percentages

	Balance score[a]	More important	Same as previously	Less important	Do not know	Total (n)
International Trade Union Confederation	8	22	53	14	11	100 (189)
European Trade Union Confederation	25	33	51	8	8	100 (194)
Global Union Federations[b]	38	47	36	9	8	100 (194)
National Trade Union Confederation	42	47	46	5	2	100 (202)
European Trade Union Federations[c]	51	57	31	6	6	100 (214)

[a]Balance score = More important − Less important
[b]E.g., BWI, IndustriALL Global, ITF, PSI, UNI-Global
[c]E.g., EFBWW, ETF, EPSU, IndustriALL Europe, UNI-Europa
Source Own data, survey 2

during the ten years before 2015–2016. Only a few stated that there had been a decrease in the significance of any of the meta-organizations mentioned and, with the exception for the ITUC, the balance scores are strongly positive. The ETUFs show the largest increase during this 10-year period. Over half (57%) of the unions declared that the ETUFs had become more important, which is a higher proportion than the increase in importance of their own national trade union confederation (47%), the GUFs (47%), the ETUC (33%) and the ITUC (22%).

Even though all listed meta-organizations seem to have become more important over time, sectoral-level cooperation turned out to have increased the most. In addition to the figures in Table 2.2, 74% of the responding unions affirmed that for the future their organization would prefer to have more transnational cooperation in their own sector rather than more cooperation with unions in other sectors in their own country.

These results should be interpreted with some caution, though, since they are based on responses from unions below the peak level only, and since non-respondents may include disproportionately large numbers of unions with little interest in European cooperation. Nevertheless, it is difficult to overlook that data are in line with the institutional development at European level discussed in Chapter 1—that the sectoral level has been attributed greater importance by the European Commission since 1998, when a reform was carried out to strengthen and advance negotiations between unions and employers within the framework of ESSD committees (Rhodes 2015; cf. Degryse 2015; Prosser 2016).

To understand better in what ways the ETUFs have increased in importance, it is necessary to distinguish some of their main functions. Schematically, union cooperation through the meta-organizations of both the ETUC and the ETUFs can be said to have three main purposes: (1) to coordinate national strategies through exchanges of information, arrangements of training, and coordination of trade union action; (2) to influence EU policies and legislation through lobbying and consultation in various committees and organs; and (3) to deliver common statements and agreements through social dialogues and negotiations with European employer organizations, both at cross-sectoral and industry level. Coordination, lobbying and negotiations actually exist simultaneously within the social dialogues.

In survey 2, we listed a number of statements on the ESSD and asked respondents to indicate to what extent they agreed. Since it requires quite some resources to take part in such joint work at European level, we included a couple of items on whether respondents thought that such collaboration really benefited the interests of their members and workers in general and whether they hesitated to participate because of the costs in time and resources (Table 2.3).

As shown in Table 2.3, there was strong recognition from the surveyed trade unions that the ESSD is important, not only to negotiate with employer organizations, but also to influence the European Commission and, especially, to strengthen transnational union cooperation. It was also commonly seen as crucial to meet the interests of members nationally. On all of these statements, not far from 80% up to nearly 90% of the responding unions agreed to some or a high degree and hence we find high summary indicators. As noted in Chapter 1, most of the outcomes of the ESSDs are non-binding declarations, joint statements, procedural documents or soft guidelines. Against that background, it might perhaps be surprising that about 77% of the unions agreed to some or a high degree in that the ESSD has a crucial role to meet the interests of workers and more than 50% did the same regarding whether it had had great significance for the employment and working conditions of their members. On the latter statement, however, the proportion being hesitant was substantial. There was even more scepticism regarding whether the dialogues actually deliver in relation to the efforts put in. 37% of the respondents leaned towards doubting whether it was in fact worth the effort, given the time and resources required to take part in meetings, committees and working groups related to the ESSD. Still, the summary indicator is negative (note that the statement goes in the opposite direction compared to the others in the table).

The last thing to consider as concerns the transnational meta-organizations in Europe is that there exists an additional level based on supranational organizations in some regions. These are very varied, and the strongest institutionalized form of cooperation—that is, joint formal and staffed meta-organizations at both sectoral and cross-sectoral levels—is present as far as we know only in the Nordic countries.[1] Moreover, the Nordic confederations have relations with the Baltic States,

Table 2.3 Trade unions' agreement on various statements on the ESSD. Percentages

	Summary indicator[a]	To a high degree	To some degree	To a low degree	Not at all	Do not know	Total (n)
It is important for strengthening transnational trade union cooperation	80	43	46	8	1	2	100 (211)
It is important for influencing EU policies	72	40	45	9	4	2	100 (209)
It is important for negotiations with European employer's associations	58	40	37	15	4	4	100 (208)
It plays a crucial role for trade unions to meet the interests of workers	56	41	36	19	2	2	100 (211)
It has had great significance for the employment and working conditions for our members	12	20	34	32	10	4	100 (208)
As it takes time and resources, we doubt whether participation is worth the effort	−23	10	27	30	30	3	100 (207)

[a]Summary indicator = (To a high degree + To some degree) − (To a low degree + Not at all)
Source Own data, survey 2

whose federations may exchange observers at meetings. There is also cooperation through the Baltic Organizing Academy and the Baltic Sea Trade Union Network. The cooperation is rather unilateral, consisting of targeted support given from Nordic to Baltic unions. These asymmetric relationships have a long tradition, but we find a certain resignation among the Nordic respondents concerning the changes in the Baltics. The development was said to be very slow and to yield quite meagre results in terms of member recruitment and organizational capacities. Overall, the differences in the Nordic unions' bilateral relations with 'core' countries in Central/Western and Western Europe and with the Baltic States respectively show the importance of organizational strength among cooperating partners. With weak partners, the relationship becomes asymmetrical and unidirectional in the flow of information and resources and thereby less useful compared to collaboration with stronger unions in Central/Western and Western Europe.

Networks of Bi- and Multilateral Cooperation

Besides the meta-organizations in Europe, there are also less formalized and institutionalized cooperation structures. These often take the form of direct bi- or multilateral communication and coordination networks between national unions. From the theoretical assumptions, the existence of formal Nordic meta-organizations may be seen as both being based on and further facilitating informal collaboration in the region. A particular feature of the Nordic cooperation seems to be its high internal synchronization compared to other areas in Europe. Through their relatively strong cultural community and similarities in traditions, Nordic trade unions have built a strong foundation of trust, which allows them a rapid response from each other when wanted, for example to obtain information or to provide support through solidarity action.

The strong Nordic coordination makes unions well-prepared for meetings in the ETUC and the ETUFs, in which they often speak with one voice (Seeliger 2019: 111–112, 169–170). When working as a coalition through the Council of Nordic Trade Unions, in relation to the ETUC they were—at least some years ago—the third largest formally organized

2 Patterns of Transnational Trade Union Cooperation in Europe

and staffed coalition of national unions after the British Trade Union Confederation and the German DGB Confederation (Degryse and Tilly 2013: 73). The Nordic meta-organizations also facilitate direct, bilateral cooperation from below and have a brokerage function in collaboration with other important European trade unions. From our interviews, it seems that this mediation is most developed in the metal sector; a quote from a union representative from Sweden gives a picture of this:

> [Our Nordic Sector Federation] has a formal arrangement with the Germans, in that our chairmen … meet the leaders of the German federations… We have meetings… at… international secretary level, with the British [and] with the French. Not so much [with] the Spanish yet, and not so much [with] Italians, but on and off … [with Eastern Europe] it is also a bit more ad hoc, and happens especially in connection with meetings [in] IndustriAll Europe.

In many regions in Europe, there are of course loose bilateral and multilateral communication and coordination networks, through which unions exchange information for use at national level. To some extent, these networks are connected to the ETUFs, in the form of organized sub-groupings based on geographical proximity. This is not always the case, though, and hence such regional networks have varying levels of organization and strength. An Italian representative of a union in the construction sector offered the following depiction:

> Europe is more or less divided in areas: We have the Nordic part; the Nordic federation in the EFBWW… Then we have a predominant area, in the centre of Europe—I mean Germany, Austria, and Switzerland… and, some years ago, maybe nine, ten years, we established a sort of coordination group within the Southern Europe area. It is composed of Italy, Spain, Portugal and Belgium—who wants to be with us. We meet regularly five, six times per year and, yeah, we have a sort of coordination.

To this listing of more or less organized networks, a Czech unionist added the extended Visegrad group, including unions from Germany, Poland, Slovakia, Hungary, Austria and the Czech Republic and with interest from Swiss unions to take part: 'All representatives from this group meet once a year at least, and we inform each other about trade union activities in these countries and discuss different topics within our sectors'. Compared to the more organized metal sector, the international network structures in the other sectors studied seem to have been built very much from below, albeit in relation to the ETUF structures. An Italian representative of a union in the hospital sector gave an example of this, talking about an informal alliance in Southern Europe:

> We have a… Mediterranean group. This is a self-organized network by the trade unions in Portugal, Spain, Italy, Greece, and France. Not part of the group but part of its work [are] Cyprus, Malta, and Israel… I say it is self-organized because the meetings are paid for by the trade unions… We work together in terms of web-networking or meeting once a year. We exchange all the information that we need on all the sectors [within EPSU].

This regional clustering of networks has been confirmed in our quantitative and social network analyses (Larsson and Törnberg 2019; Vulkan and Larsson 2019). In survey 2, respondents were asked about the 3–5 most important regular cooperation partners. The analyses disclosed that such networks tended to be concentrated in their own sector. The reason is a combination of from-below interest coordination and from-above organization, founded on shared sectoral interests (Bechter et al. 2012). In addition, the ESSDs and the ETUFs function as both multi-cooperation arenas for making contacts and building trust for direct inter-organizational networking.

From comparisons based on the regime typology in Chapter 1, we identified a significant tendency that bilateral union cooperation was focused on partners within the same geographical region. This confirms the patterns revealed both in qualitative research of trade union networking (Gollbach and Schulten 2000; Magnusson and Murhem 2009; Marginson and Sisson 2004: 112–113) and in Nordin's (2009) quantitative studies of the metal sector. The explanation is of course that countries within the same region are neighbours, with geographical proximity and sometimes common borders. Also institutional similarities and differences, as discussed in Chapter 1, play a role. It is obvious that industrial relations institutions (Visser et al. 2009), economic and political contexts and challenges (Gumbrell-McCormick and Hyman 2013), trade union resources (Lehndorff et al. 2017) and cultural aspects such as language, traditions, and ideology (Hyman 2001) vary with regions in Europe.

As regards regional variation, a recurrent feature in the sectors studied—metal, transport, construction, healthcare and banking and finance—is that the Central/Western European unions tended to cluster in the core of networks, whereas unions from the other regions usually gathered more peripherally—as offshoots from the central core. We could also conclude that German unions occupied the central position in all sectors, not only in cross-border bargaining networks in the metal sector as has been shown previously but in transnational cooperation more generally (Nordin 2009; Traxler et al. 2008: 222; cf. Seeliger 2019: 172–174). German unions were the main brokers between the more peripheral clusters, even though there were also some secondary brokers from other large countries in Europe.

When examining network ties, we found some differences and similarities between the regimes/regions in their balance of intra- versus interregional networking. The results of the analysis of whether a union (source) mentioned another union (target) as cooperation partner are presented in Table 2.4. As can be seen, the Nordic unions were quite intra-regionally focused, with a strong majority of their cooperation relations going to other Nordic unions. The Southern European labour organizations also had quite a strong tendency towards such an intra-regional concentration, whereas in Central/Western and Central/Eastern Europe there was a more equal balance in the selection of partners, with a greater share of cooperation links stretching out to other regions.

Looking at these results from a historical development perspective, we discover both path dependency and change. The intra-regional focus among the Nordic unions relates to their history of strong internal cooperation and possibly to their history of being somewhat reluctant Europeans as well (Seeliger 2019: 211, 226; cf. Larsson 2014, 2015). The Central/Eastern and Southern European clusters have developed more slowly and later. In the former case this was linked to the EU's enlargement to the East; the trade unions there are more fragmented and have a tendency to be more dependent on unions outside their

Table 2.4 Intra- and cross-regional ties in trade union cooperation networks. Percentages (ties $n = 487$)

Source region	Target region				
	Central/Eastern Europe	Central/Western Europe	Nordic countries	Southern Europe	Western Europe	Total (n)
Central/Eastern Europe	**49**	24	9	14	3	100 (164)
Central/Western Europe	6	**45**	4	41	4	100 (69)
Nordic countries	3	9	**82**	1	6	100 (189)
Southern Europe	–	27	3	**62**	8	100 (63)
Western Europe	–	(50)	(50)	–	–	(100) (2)

Source Own data, survey 2

own region (Léonard et al. 2012; Seeliger 2019: 211–212). The Central/Western European labour organizations early developed cooperative networks in border regions. They cluster in the core of the sector networks and they are number one concerning links to other regional clusters. The explanation is partly their resources and influential position in Europe. Another factor is that cooperation networks tend to concentrate around border regions and Central/Western European countries, taken together, border all other regions in Europe (Gollbach and Schulten 2000; Traxler et al. 2008).

Our social network analysis confirms previous research indicating that cooperation density is especially high within the metal sector (Glassner and Pusch 2013; Magnusson and Murhem 2009). The construction sector is highly integrated as well, whereas transport and healthcare have lower levels of direct transnational networking. The results found in the latter sectors have to do with the greater fragmentation in terms of occupational or sub-sectoral unions, leading to more isolated cliques in the network.

Forms of Cooperation

The presentation above is very much focused on trade unions' general views on cooperation and the multilevel structures through which cooperation is pursued. We now turn to the more concrete forms of collaboration that unions have been engaged in—from producing joint statements to concerting common actions such as demonstrations or strikes across countries.

Through the ETUC and the ETUFs and the social dialogues coordinated via these meta-organizations, unions produce a great number of resolutions, positions, petitions, open letters, etc. Some are joint statements with employer organizations on employment relations and political and economic developments in Europe. The ETUC and the ETUFs also coordinate exchange of information, for example on collective bargaining and union actions across countries. In the period before our surveys were conducted, the ETUC organized European demonstrations, both in specific cities and coordinated across different cities (Degryse and Tilly 2013). In 2012, the organization even mobilized simultaneous strikes in four countries—Italy, Greece, Portugal and Spain—as a protest against the austerity measures following the economic and financial crisis in Europe. This was however something of an exception, because strikes are generally dealt with as national matters. As for the ETUFs, we can observe quite similar palettes of activities, varying between sectors. At the level further below, we find a great variety of bi- and multilateral actions, for example exchange of information or observers in collective bargaining, cooperation around training programmes, negotiations about plant restructuring, participation in demonstrations and sympathy strikes.

To get an overview of trade unions' involvement in joint activities, we questioned respondents in both surveys about these things (Furåker and Bengtsson 2013). The results in survey 1 showed that most of the labour organizations (92%) exchanged information on collective agreements, either on a regular or a more sporadic basis. Over two-thirds (71%) of them collaborated on training programmes for union officials. More than half of the unions (52%) engaged in coordinating negotiations on plant restructuring and closures—regarding issues such as redundancies, wages and training—and more than a third (38%) exchanged observers or negotiators in collective bargaining.

Transnational action can be coordinated either through the European meta-organizations—the ETUC and the ETUFs—or in the cooperation structures existing globally above these, or regionally below them. Table 2.5 shows the responding unions' participation in actions of transnational kind as organized by the ETUC, the ETUFs and other bodies during the last three years. It also tells us something about the balance between softer and more contentious forms of action. The majority (80%) had participated in writing statements, petitions and open letters. Slightly over half (56%) of them had been involved in demonstrations and boycotts across borders and almost a fifth of the organizations stated that they had taken part in more contentious forms of action such as overtime bans, strikes or blockades with cross-border reach.

Since the greatest variation emerged in the demonstration and boycotts category, we carried out a more detailed analysis of it, showing quite large regional and sector differences (Larsson 2014). The main results

2 Patterns of Transnational Trade Union Cooperation in Europe

Table 2.5 Participation in European trade union activities during the last three years. Percentages (n = 250)

Organized by	Statements, petitions, or open letters	Demonstrations or boycotts	Overtime bans	Strikes or blockades	Sympathy strikes
ETUC	52	46	4	3	3
ETUFs (EIFs)	49	32	4	5	6
Other	29	15	3	4	3
Any of the above	80	56		18[a]	

[a] Any of the three activities "Overtime bans", "Strikes or blockades" or "Sympathy strikes"
Source Own data, survey 1

were that the Central/Western and Southern European unions had much higher degrees of participation in transnational demonstrations and boycotts than unions from the other regions, and the Nordic organizations had the lowest level of participation. Cross-sectoral peak-level confederations turned out to have more cooperation than all sectoral trade unions, with the exception of transport that obviously had organized several activities across borders during the three-year period before the survey was conducted in 2011–2012. When examining the role of size—which was used as a proxy for resources—large organizations quite unsurprisingly showed more participation in cross-border demonstrations and boycotts than smaller ones.

We also performed a similar analysis of the trade unions' views on the importance to engage more in cross-national demonstrations, boycotts, overtime bans and strikes in the future (Larsson 2014). This revealed that peak-level confederations were particularly inclined to have more of these things in the future, as were unions from Central/Western and Southern Europe compared to unions from Central/Eastern Europe and the Nordic countries. This suggests that differences in national-level industrial relations traditions affect the way cross-national activities are approached.

In order to get a deeper understanding of these activities at sectoral level, we had a similar question in survey 2, while extending the period to five years and also examining the extent to which such cooperation had taken place at national level. The purpose was to explore the balance between national and international cooperation. The results are shown in Table 2.6 and for comparative reasons we add a column with the corresponding results from survey 1 in which peak-level confederations were included.

Some main points can be drawn attention to from these results. Sectoral unions had had a great deal of cooperation with other unions in their own countries, but we also find high figures for cooperation with unions abroad in the same sector. Both more contentious forms of action such as boycotts and strikes and coordination of collective bargaining remained highly nation-based activities. Softer activities—like exchange of information on collective bargaining, authoring joint statements, petitions or open letters and organizing training—were more transnational.

2 Patterns of Transnational Trade Union Cooperation in Europe

Table 2.6 Participation in specified forms of cooperation during the past five years. Percentages[a] ($n = 221$)

	Other trade unions in own country	Trade unions abroad in same sector	Trade unions abroad in other sectors	None of these	Survey 1[b]
Joint statements, petitions, open letters	73	63	18	5	79
Information on collective agreements	67	75	24	5	92
Demonstrations	64	47	23	15	56
Coordination of collective bargaining	58	31	5	22	n.a.
Training of union officials	54	53	17	15	71
Boycotts, overtime bans or strikes	48	18	7	31	18
Exchange of observers or negotiators in collective bargaining	28	25	5	41	38

[a] It was possible to tick more than one alternative; thus the percentages add up to more than 100. 'Do not know' is not reported in the table
[b] 'Participation in European trade union action during last three years' ($n = 250$)
Sources Own data, survey 1 and 2

In addition, the second survey suggests that sectoral trade unions had somewhat lower degrees of cooperation than peak-level confederations, which can be seen in that the numbers in the second column of figures are mostly lower than those from survey 1 in the last column. It is also worth noting that, if ranked, the levels of transnational cooperation in the two forms mentioned are consistent across the two surveys.

As there was quite great variation in the extent to which unions cooperated transnationally, we created an index of all the relevant forms to measure the overall level of cooperation. This aimed at studying whether regime and sector differences and the resources of a union (i.e., size) could explain the patterns (Vulkan and Larsson 2019). The regression results (not shown) indicated that the size of organizations was strongly significant: the larger the union, the more of transnational cooperation. We did not find any markedly strong differences across industrial relations regimes/regions, but some significant sectoral dissimilarity became visible. Labour organizations in the services industry were, on average, less engaged in various forms of cooperation than those in other sectors. Unions in the metal sector were involved in most forms of cooperation, and unions in transport and construction as well as trans-sectoral unions had an intermediate position.

Channels for Influencing EU Policies

One important reason for trade unions to cooperate transnationally in Europe is their interest in influencing the development of EU policies and regulations. In Chapter 1, we identified the different access points in this respect through social dialogues, consultations in various committees and fora and joint lobbying. Besides these channels there are national routes as well to influence the EU. Unions may, for example, lobby their own national members of the European parliament and they may try to have some bearing on their own government's position in the Council or other fora to impact on policy development (Clauwaert 2011; Greenwood 2007: 127–130; cf. Larsson 2015).

When, in survey 1, asked about whom their trade union cooperated with to influence EU policies, it turned out that the national route was

2 Patterns of Transnational Trade Union Cooperation in Europe 53

very important for unions. 75% of the responding unions stated that they collaborated to some or to a high degree with national authorities and political parties to achieve this kind of influence (Table 2.7). In contrast, the least important route was other NGOs or networks, with only 34% of the labour organizations indicating that they cooperated with these to the same degree. The ETUFs, the trade unions' own Brussels offices, the ETUC, various cross-national regional networks and members of political groups in the European parliament were on average ranked in between.

To understand the variation in how trade unions cooperate to affect EU policies and what channels they use to do that, we elaborated the analysis somewhat further. We created an index of the overall usage of different channels, by adding the seven items in Table 2.7, and run regressions with industrial relations regimes/regions, sectors and size of the organization as independent variables to explain differences (Larsson 2015). The results confirmed that there was more cooperation to influence the EU among larger unions than among smaller ones. Additionally, collaboration was somewhat less in services than in manufacturing, transport and construction and it was highest among the peak confederations. In terms of regimes or regions, the Central/Western European unions had the highest levels of overall cooperation. The Western and Central/Eastern European labour organizations had the lowest levels, while the Nordic and the Southern European unions appeared in a middle position.

Furthermore, we examined the balance between what we categorized as 'own channels' and 'cooperative channels' to affect EU policies. The former is defined as trade unions' cooperation through their own national government, political parties or the national Brussels offices and the latter category means cooperation within the ETUC and the ETUFs. As shown in Fig. 2.2, we placed the zero point (intercept) in the balance score at 0.3, which was the mean of the total. This indicates a slight overall tendency that unions collaborated more through their own channels (positive numbers in balance score) than through the cooperative channels (negative numbers).

Central/Western European unions can be said to make up sort of a benchmark for the others: they not only had the highest degree of cooperation to influence EU policies, but also deviated the least from the

Table 2.7 Trade unions' channels of cooperation to influence EU policies. Means and percentages (n = 241)

	Means[a]	To a high degree	To some degree	To a low degree	Not at all	n[b]
National authorities or political parties	3.02	32	43	19	5	228
ETUFs	2.81	38	27	12	23	212
Trade union offices in Brussels	2.67	26	34	22	19	209
ETUC	2.59	22	35	25	18	224
Cross-national/regional union networks	2.51	22	31	22	24	212
Members of political groups in the European parliament	2.43	15	35	27	22	227
Other NGOs or networks	2.09	8	26	33	33	219

[a]Range 1–4: 1 = 'not important at all'; 2 = 'rather unimportant'; 3 = 'rather important'; 4 = 'very important'
[b]'Do not know' is recoded as missing
Source Own data, survey 1. The nine ETUFs were excluded from these analyses

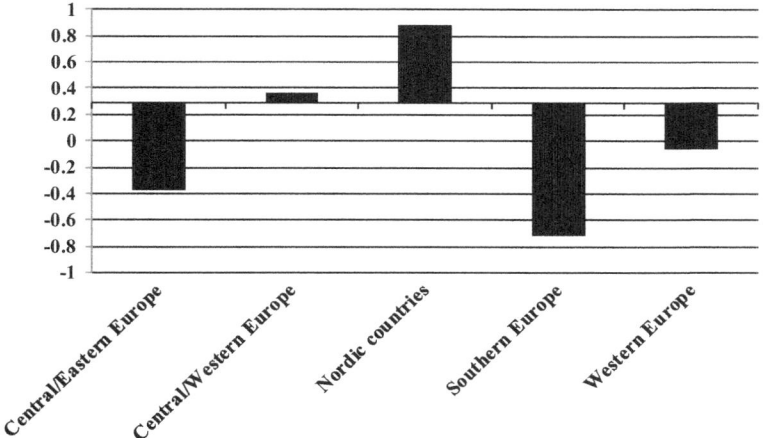

Fig. 2.2 Balance scores[a] on own channels vs. cooperative channels, by region ($n = 209–228$)
[a]Balance scores range from 1 to −1. They are based on the means on the first four items in Table 2.7 (National authorities or political parties + Trade union offices in Brussels) − (ETUFs + ETUC). 'Do not know' is recoded as missing
Source Own data, survey 1

overall balance between collaboration through their own channels and the cooperative channels through the ETUC and the ETUFs. In comparison, we see that the Nordic unions tended to orient themselves more to the first alternative than to the second, whereas the Southern (in particular) and the Central Eastern European unions had the contrary tendency to emphasize cooperation through the meta-organizations.

Focus and Topics of Cooperation

The analyses above make clear that some of the differences in the forms and intensity of cooperation are related to differences in industrial relations regimes/regions, sectors and organizational resources. However, trade unions also face quite varying challenges because of specific political and economic developments at both national and sectoral/industry level (Gumbrell-McCormick and Hyman 2013: 37–46). Thus, they cannot be expected to be interested or engaged in cooperation around the same general issues or topics. We bring up a couple of examples of this in the case studies following in Chapters 3 and 4, but already in the current section we give a brief overview of what topics and issues that unions in different sectors and countries considered important to collaborate on nationally and transnationally.

In survey 2, we questioned the union representatives about both their existing cooperation on a number of different issues and how important they found them to be for the future. Before going into the details, we can note that the overall results in Table 2.8 verify some of the findings presented above. There was a higher prevalence of national compared with transnational collaboration and most of the latter was focused on trade unions in the same sector. The outcomes also confirm that most unions were engaged in some cooperation, either national or transnational (Vulkan and Larsson 2019).

By looking at the differences between the levels of existing cooperation with other unions in their own country and cooperation with foreign unions in the same sector, we discover some broad tendencies in Table 2.8. Wages were not surprisingly a very nationally based issue. The topics of unemployment/employment, working time, and employment protection legislation had a similar tendency to be nationally oriented, but to a lesser extent. In contrast, migration and recruitment of members tended to be similarly strong in transnational cooperation. At the same time, these are topics on which approximately 30–40% of the responding unions indicated no cooperation at all.

Regarding how important the topics were believed to be for future transnational cooperation (column on the far right), the results indicate that topics on which unions already cooperated were seen as the most important. Still, there are some exceptions to this. When comparing how high the different issues were ranked (in percentages and means), we find that the category of professional matters seems to be given less weight for the future compared to existing levels of cooperation. Similarly and more significantly, two of the absolute core issues for trade unions, wages and working hours, were perceived as more important for future cooperation in comparison with existing cooperation on these topics. This may be a reaction to the consequences of the financial crisis when many labour organizations in Europe had to accept wage and working time

Table 2.8 Trade union cooperation on various topics during the past five years. Percentages[a] ($n = 221$)

	Other trade unions in country	Trade unions abroad in same sector	Trade unions abroad in other sectors	None of these	Future importance (means[b])
Employment protection legislation	76	45	16	12	2.82
Occupational health and safety	75	56	19	10	2.92
Wages	68	34	7	24	2.52
Unemployment/employment	67	40	12	22	2.50
Professional issues	67	55	9	13	2.41
Working time	66	43	12	20	2.74
Public services cuts/austerity measures	53	33	15	32	2.22
Migration	41	45	15	34	2.42
Recruitment of members	39	36	6	41	2.23

[a]It was possible to tick more than one alternative; thus the percentages add up to more than 100. 'Do not know' is not reported in the table

[b]Range 1–4: 1 = 'not important at all'; 2 = 'rather unimportant'; 3 = 'rather important'; 4 = 'very important'. 'Do not know' is coded as missing

Source Own data, survey 2

reductions. It may also signal that respondents believed that such questions—which are still nationally bound—would need to be discussed more across Europe (Dribbusch et al. 2017; Müller and Platzer 2017). One critical part of the European-level cooperation on wages has to do with the minimum wage issue, to which we will come back in Chapter 3.

We ran regressions to examine the effects of industrial relations regimes/regions, sectors and the size of organizations on all these items (Vulkan and Larsson 2019). Previous outcomes were substantiated, indicating that size played a clear role for the level of transnational cooperation and that unions in the services sector normally cooperated less than unions in the other sectors. When it comes to the selection of specific topics to work on, sectoral differences turned out to have a greater part than industrial relation regimes/regions. This is not very unexpected, because the challenges that trade unions and their members meet vary with sectoral and industry-specific conditions. Labour organizations in construction showed an especially strong tendency to focus on occupational health and safety and migration issues. Unions organizing public sector employees, particularly in healthcare, cooperated more than others on the topic of public services cuts/austerity measures. Likewise, unions in the metal sector directed more attention than others to cooperation around unemployment/employment.

Obstacles to Cooperation

Given the views regarding the importance and benefits of transnational cooperation and the extent of existing collaboration through networks and meta-organizations, one might wonder whether unions believe that everything is good enough already. The answer must in spite of this be 'no', insofar as many of them stated that more cross-border activities would be desirable. Therefore we want to take a closer look at what factors that hinder and facilitate cooperation.

To begin with obstacles, we asked unions to rate to what degree different factors hindered union cooperation in Europe. The response patterns appear in Table 2.9. The items are ranked by the total means and the first

Table 2.9 Perceived obstacles to trade union cooperation. Means[a]

	Total	Central/Eastern Europe	Central/Western Europe	Nordic countries	Southern Europe	Western Europe
Differences in financial resources among unions	3.04	3.53	3.07	2.99	2.89	2.78
Diversity of labour market policies and regulations	2.88	2.97	2.75	2.93	2.97	2.61
Low priority among union leaders	2.84	2.81	2.60	2.89	2.94	2.92
Employers' 'divide-and-rule' strategies	2.80	3.28	2.98	2.47	3.08	2.61
Low interest among union members	2.80	2.87	2.88	2.70	2.89	2.88
Differences in leaders' mother tongue and language skills	2.75	3.09	2.86	2.62	2.95	2.27
Competition between high- and low-wage countries	2.71	3.25	2.64	2.61	2.73	2.52
Diversity in ideological/political/religious orientations	2.65	2.20	2.61	2.76	2.83	2.57
Differences in union membership rates	2.64	2.66	2.63	2.68	2.66	2.41
Differences in national cultures and traditions	2.51	2.39	2.41	2.65	2.44	2.36
n	215–234	29–32	43–44	88–100	35–37	18–24

[a]Range 1–4: 1 = 'not important at all'; 2 = 'rather unimportant'; 3 = 'rather important'; 4 = 'very important'. 'Do not know/no opinion' is coded as missing, which explains the variation in n. For detailed PCA and regression analyses, see Larsson (2012, 2017)

Source Own data, survey 1

column of figures shows that differences in financial resources were generally regarded as the greatest obstacle of the ten factors listed, while differences in national cultures and traditions were considered least important. Yet, even the last in ranking gets a total mean of 2.51 on a scale ranging from 1 to 4. In other words, cultural factors were not regarded as unimportant, only less so than other factors. A general conclusion from Table 2.9 could be that cross-border trade union cooperation has many difficulties to defeat to develop positively.

From the compared means analysis in the following columns—and originally tested in regressions (Larsson 2017)—we find marked variations in how some of these obstacles were weighed by trade unions in different industrial relations regimes/regions. Central/Eastern European organizations underscored difficulties with financial resources, competition between high- and low-wage countries, and employer organizations' power strategies. Also Southern European unions seemed to deem the latter to be a problem, but this result was not statistically significant in the regressions. Nordic unions attributed employers' power strategies to be clearly less important. We also discovered some significant differences in the means on the three items related to culture. Compared to other organizations, particularly those from the Central/Eastern Europe, Western European unions regarded language issues to be less of an obstacle. Difficulties based on ideological, political or religious diversity were highlighted by Southern European respondents, while being viewed as slightly less problematic by Central/Eastern European unions. Finally, the Nordic unions rated differences in national cultures and traditions somewhat higher as a barrier than did unions from the other regions. Once again, the largest sectoral difference was that between, on the one hand, labour organizations in manufacturing and construction emphasizing resources and, on the other hand, those representing services and professional groups stressing members' low prioritization and interest as an obstacle to cross-border cooperation (Larsson 2012).

The interviews largely confirmed that differences in financial resources—and especially the lack of resources among small unions and unions in Central/Eastern Europe—were a great problem for cooperation. It is also a dilemma for those with more resources, when their poorer partners cannot take part. The difficulty of prioritizing working at European level—in light of the lacking interest among members—was touched upon in the interviews too. It connects to the balance between the logic of influence and the logic of membership. Differences in labour market policy and regulations have varying implications in different sectors. Whereas in healthcare it was frequently a matter of diverse financing systems and educational requirements across Europe, in manufacturing the discussion was about competition related to wage differentials and more or less explicit strategies of governments to support certain industries. At a more general level, divergences in the regulations of working conditions and the wage-setting processes make it difficult to reach an understanding of what to aim for with cooperation in the ETUC and the ETUFs—an issue to which we come back in the analysis of the minimum wage issue in Chapter 3. Cultural factors were talked about quite extensively in the interviews, which is why we return to them immediately after paying attention to some of the facilitators for trade union cooperation.

Factors Facilitating Cooperation

If the above are some of the most important obstacles to transnational union cooperation, are there corresponding facilitators and, if so, which are they? It may seem likely that these comprise ways to overcome the existing barriers related to resources, institutional differences, low priorities, resistance to European-level social dialogue from employers, etc. For the purpose of validating the question on obstacles, we inquired about the importance of a number of factors for union cooperation in Europe to become successful (Table 2.10).

The results presented in Table 2.10 back up some of the outcomes regarding the obstacles to cooperation. From the means we can draw the conclusion that cultural factors had less weight than similarities in labour market policies and regulation, similarities in occupational interests and well-developed personal networks and relations between trade union leaders. The three culture-related items were, more or less, ranked in the same way as they were as obstacles: language was considered more

Table 2.10 Factors considered important for trade unions' successful transnational cooperation. Means[a]

	Total	Central/Eastern Europe	Central/Western Europe	Nordic region	Southern Europe	Western Europe
Similarities in labour market policies and regulations	3.28	3.41	3.26	3.28	3.37	3.04
Similarities in occupational interests among unions	3.25	3.34	3.16	3.20	3.18	3.65
Union leaders' personal networks and relations	3.24	3.44	3.42	3.19	3.21	2.87
Union leaders' mother tongue and language skills	2.81	3.26	2.88	2.75	2.66	2.57
Similarities in ideological, political and religious orientations	2.60	2.40	2.57	2.70	2.40	2.83
Similarities in national cultures and traditions	2.47	2.61	2.48	2.54	2.17	2.48
n	225–232	28–31	42–43	96–100	34–35	23–24

[a]Range 1–4: 1 = 'not important at all'; 2 = 'rather unimportant'; 3 = 'rather important'; 4 = 'very important'. 'Do not know/no opinion' is coded as missing, which explains the variation in n. For detailed PCA and regression analyses, see Larsson (2012, 2017)

Source Own data, survey 1

important than similarities in ideological, political or religious orientations and similarities in national cultures and traditions came last among the six factors listed.

Just as on the impediments to cooperation, we find some significant differences in means when comparing industrial relations regimes/regions (Larsson 2017). Central/Eastern and Western European unions scored higher on the importance of similarities of occupational interests between unions. Further, Western European respondents put markedly less weight on the role of personal networks than did respondents from the other regimes. If these two results are somewhat puzzling, the outcomes on cultural factors are noticeably more in line with the previous analysis of how obstacles were perceived. Central/Eastern European unions, which had the highest score on language as a barrier to cooperation, also emphasized the significance of language skills for successful cooperation. The Nordic labour organizations highlighted the value of similar ideological, political and religious orientations—as did those from Western Europe. Finally, the Southern European trade unions were relatively less inclined to stress similarities in national culture and traditions for successful transnational union cooperation.

Cultural Obstacles to Cooperation

We now turn to the interview study to specify the cultural obstacles to transnational trade union cooperation in Europe—what problems exist, how and why cultural differences create problems and what cultural borders the respondents identified within Europe. The analysis is linked to the previous quantitative investigation in that the three surveyed cultural factors will be treated in the order of importance, as uncovered by results above. First, we look at how and why language differences create problems. Then the focus is on obstacles related to unions' ideological, political or religious orientations. Finally, we bring up what the interviews tell us about the role of differences and borders between national cultures.

The interviews verified that differences in mother tongue and lack of foreign language skills were considered great obstacles (Larsson 2017, 2020). Especially Central/Eastern European respondents saw language barriers as 'strong', 'essential', 'huge' or even as 'the major obstacle' (cf. Henning 2015a). Some interviewees from the English- and German-speaking countries found these barriers to be less of a problem, since good translations and interpretations exist. Others, however, acknowledged the language difficulties, as for instance in this quotation from a British unionist:

> We're very lucky because [we're] English… In fact, some of our ETUF meetings are only conducted in English, so that can be a barrier for other organizations… Some people come and they never say anything. And then other organizations, they can only send someone who is quite good at speaking English.

The ETUC and ETUF congresses normally admit funding for up to six language interpretations. At committee meetings, there are fewer interpretations, while seminars and working groups are typically held in English only, forcing participants to speak 'some kind of joint bad English'. This is problematic since some participants do not have the skills and others are unwilling even to try to speak the meeting language. Those lacking English skills thus have to forgo or bring their own interpreters (cf. Henning 2015a). Interpretation is not uncomplicated either, because the precision or even the very substance may get lost in translation. Terms and concepts are embedded in, and always refer to, a cognitive (and often normative) content and a common world of reference (Barbier 2013: 109; cf. Hyman 2004). As a consequence, there are difficulties of the kind mentioned as expressed by an Italian union representative (Larsson 2020: 7):

> The Nordic countries [have] a different understanding of what 'austerity' means; what 'crisis' in the public sector means… You need to build a common vocabulary … to understand what the others are saying. And if the words are different—like 'privatisation' or 'public sector' or what the meaning is of 'autonomous', 'independent'… This is the major obstacle.

Translations of central documents may create problems too, because there can be misunderstandings due to differences in connotations of concepts. These linguistic problems are not only costly and hamper

2 Patterns of Transnational Trade Union Cooperation in Europe 65

understanding, but they also reduce the possibility for some unions to influence the discussion. These organizations are forced to choose between having representatives staying silent or sending representatives on the basis of their language skills rather than their expertise. An illustration of this is taken from a Latvian interviewee (Larsson 2020: 7):

> If we have two or three people who are capable of speaking in English, the same people have to be competent in various themes and specific subjects, and it is very hard to do that at a good level... It is very hard to come out with an argument or a competent opinion of things.

The absence of a common language tends to make overall trust building harder as well since small talk becomes more difficult. Some union representatives asserted that it is in small talk that joint ideas are developed and that 'the real business gets done in the meeting beforehand or over lunch'.

Trade unions also differ in their ideological, political and religious orientations and it is well known that such differences can create problems for collaboration. As discussed in Chapter 1, some are more of 'business unions' mainly representing their members' interests as cartels, while others are more political or 'movement unions' trying to represent the interests of the working class or workers in general (Gumbrell-McCormick and Hyman 2013: 6–28; Henning 2015b; Hyman 2001). Moreover, there are organizations adhering to radical leftist political ideas, reformist and consensus-oriented unions and those that are more on the conservative side. The deepest rift in ideology appearing in the interviews was said to go between consensus- and conflict-oriented traditions. These are not neatly grouped regionally, but a main North–South divergence was mentioned recurrently (cf. Henning 2015a; Larsson 2014). We can give an example of how it was communicated by a Spanish representative (Larsson 2020: 11):

> There is a clear division North-South. We mobilize the workers at the social and political level; we have general strikes, mass demonstrations

in the streets. The Nordic unions have collective bargaining at the sectoral level or national level… It is, therefore, not easy to establish one [common] way of trade union action at the European level.

Both other Southern European and Nordic union officials confirmed this divide between cooperating and compromising with employers versus having more conflictual and confrontational relations (cf. Lovén Seldén 2014). To some extent, the latter attitude may create misunderstandings and even disapproval. Some Nordic interviewees talked about unions in Southern Europe as being more of 'campaign organizations', which do not take their seat at the negotiating table, but instead 'go in the streets and shout'. Whereas they saw themselves as 'more constructive', they thought others would find them a bit 'wimpish', 'not passionate enough', or 'woody'. This was further supported when some Southern European representatives characterized the Nordics as 'less European' or as not being solidary.

Besides the North–South division, respondents also made comments on an East–West difference (cf. Henning 2015b). Some Central/Eastern European unions were said to have very different views, shaped by their post-communist legacy of having strong connections to political parties. Still, several interviewees acknowledged that North–South and East–West typologies were too schematic, because there are different traditions even within regions and countries—some being more homogenous and others more fragmented. The internal fragmentation of the trade union movement in some countries can, though, be taken as another aspect of cultural difficulties, implying that unions from more homogenous contexts find it difficult to cooperate with those that are not even on speaking terms within their own country (cf. Henning 2015a, b).

The factor that was attributed least importance in the survey was differences in national cultures and traditions. It is perhaps a more abstract dimension than the one on ideological, political and religious variations. There are certainly overlaps between the two dimensions, but the one of national cultures and traditions is presumably more general in character. When we—in our interviews—discussed the North–South split in Europe, we once again ran into some schematic divisions, exemplified by an Italian union representative (Larsson 2020: 8):

> It is easier for us [Italians] to have cooperation with the Mediterranean countries—I am talking about Spanish and French …because we have more or less the same culture, and it is easier for us to have good relations… When we talk with our colleagues from Scandinavia, it is complicated [for them] to understand our problems, because, you know, they are very far from us.

In a similar vein, a British respondent viewed relations with French colleagues as difficult, using the following words: '/T/hat is partly about language, but it is also about the traditions and the way they do things'. This cultural divide is linked to the ideological gap discussed above, but it was seen as going beyond ideology (Larsson 2020: 10):

> The Nordic countries are used to negotiating, the Germans are, and we [British] are… It is culture! And it is easier for us to do business with the Nordics and the Germans, because they understand, or we have a common interest in doing a deal. Whereas it seems to me—and I am aware that I am stereotyping culturally—the French and the Spanish and the Greeks in particular come to those meetings to make a point, to make a speech.

These differences appear not only in basic values and conceptions, but also in traditional everyday practices like what is expected in social situations and how one expresses oneself. They include everything from how delegates from various countries stick to the starting times of meetings to how much they talk and how they interact socially. Such things may seem trivial, but they affect the internal processes in the European organizations. One example is the difference between the more 'talkative' Southern European delegates and the more 'taciturn' Nordic, as shown in a study of speech patterns at ETUC Executive Committee meetings (Furåker and Lovén Seldén 2016). At such meetings, the Nordic delegates are coordinated through their joint organizations (Seeliger 2019: 169–170, 212–213, 226). Their position is already negotiated and they have little need to mark a unique position, as explained by a Swedish unionist: 'So we give a few statements to explain our position, and then the others get to talk'. This was said to lead to confusion and even irritation from others, who, in contrast 'must express their organization and its ideas, values and agenda', irrespective of others voicing a similar line of argument.

Cultural features are important for how the member organizations of the ETUC and the ETUFs perceive both the content and legitimacy of decisions. A representative of a joint Nordic organization suggested that the decision-making in these organizations 'does not have the same strong formalistic approach to democracy that we have here'. There is seldom any voting except in congresses and the process is rather consensus-seeking, followed by an attempt to spell out the decisions in an understandable summary—as argued by a Swedish unionist (Larsson 2020: 10):

> We have our model in Sweden—how to do it. The Germanic model: then you have the question 'Who is for; who is against; someone who abstains?' We don't do it like that here. This must be learned. If you don't, you immediately will kick up a row. And why? Because then they will not understand what they have decided… So, clearly, cultural differences make it difficult. And that is why it is necessary to understand these cultural differences… I have seen those who have failed with that. The consequence was crazy decisions—if any decisions at all.

Cultural differences can hence have quite serious consequences. They affect not only whether decisions are perceived as legitimate, but also how their content is understood—and may as a result also influence how well they are implemented.

Some cultural borders between East and West were mentioned and they were from time to time associated with the question of ideology. It was said that some Central/Eastern European societies were 'hierocracies' and 'post-communist' rather than 'democratic' (cf. Henning 2015b). This was recognized by both Western and Central/Eastern European respondents. There could, however, also be resistance to such categorization: A trade union official from Latvia emphasized that the Baltic States are not part of a Central/Eastern European culture, but have more in common with the Nordic countries. A Hungarian representative dismissed the idea of a great cultural divide, arguing that the cultural divergences in Europe were nothing compared to those between Europe and other continents:

> Today in Europe, this is no problem; more and more people work in England, Germany, Sweden. More Hungarian people work in Sweden. I think there is no distance in culture. No problem. Other nations: Asian nations, Muslim, or African nations have other cultures, but Hungary, no problem. Hungary is very, very similar to Germany. We have a lot of German companies.

This kind of relativity of cultural borders also appeared when the interviews centred on regions that are presented as culturally homogeneous. For many, the Nordic countries make up such a region, because they 'live in the same cultural world' and 'see things the same way'. Nevertheless, when viewed more closely, these similarities were sometimes dissolved. In practice, there could be cultural heterogeneity in the joint Nordic organizations (Larsson 2020: 9):

> The Danish… are very straightforward… If you are quiet, you have nothing to say, from a Danish perspective. While in Finland, it may well be that you are talking in a different way, you have a bit longer pauses and so, but if you sit in a meeting you are expected to be asked by the chairman of the meeting about what to do. And if you are not asked, you leave the meeting feeling trampled on.

It is important not to exaggerate these cultural variations and the difficulties they create for trade union cooperation. As we could see in Table 2.9, cultural differences were not perceived as the most important obstacles to cooperation. It is possible for actors to overcome many of the cultural barriers. An Italian representative stated this plainly: 'It is not easy at the very beginning. But if you participate in many meetings, during many years, you can do it'. What is more, we should not neglect the existence of solidarity across countries and the shared values in the European political culture and trade union movement (Gajewska 2009; Pernicka and

Glassner 2014). If there were nothing of this kind, union cooperation would not be possible at all.

Note

1. At cross-sectoral level, there is the Council of Nordic Trade Unions; at sectoral level in the five sectors studied, there are the Industrial Employees in the Nordic region, the Nordic Building and Woodworkers' Federation, the Nordic Transport Workers' Federation, Nordic Financial Unions and the Nordic Public Employees Trade Unions.

References

Ahrne, G., and N. Brunsson. 2008. *Meta-organizations*. Cheltenham: Edward Elgar.

Banyuls, J., T. Haipeter, and L. Neumann. 2008. European Works Council at General Motors Europe: Bargaining Efficiency in Regime Competition? *Industrial Relations Journal* 39 (6): 532–547.

Barbier, J.C. 2013. *The Road to Social Europe: A Contemporary Approach to Political Cultures and Diversity in Europe*. London: Routledge.

Bechter, B., B. Brandl, and G. Meardi. 2012. Sectors or Countries? Typologies and Levels of Analysis in Comparative Industrial Relations. *European Journal of Industrial Relations* 18 (3): 185–202.

Bengtsson, M., and P. Vulkan. 2018. After the Great Recession: Unions' Views on Transnational Interest and Cooperation. *Nordic Journal of Working Life Studies* 8 (3): 111–133.

Busemeyer, M.R., C. Kellerman, A. Petring, and A. Stuchlik. 2008. Overstreching Solidarity? Trade Unions' National Perspectives on the European Economic and Social Model. *Transfer: European Review of Labour and Research* 14 (3): 435–452.

Clauwaert, S. 2011. 2011: 20 Years of European Interprofessional Social Dialogue: Achievements and Prospects. *Transfer: European Review of Labour and Research* 17 (2): 169–179.

Degryse, C. 2015. *The European Sectoral Social Dialogue: An Uneven Record of Achievement?* Brussels: ETUI.

Degryse, C., and P. Tilly. 2013. *1973–2013: 40 Years of History of the European Trade Union Confederation*. Brussels: ETUI.

Dølvik, J.E. 1997. *Redrawing Boundaries of Solidarity? ETUC, Social Dialogue and the Europeanization of Trade Unions in the 1990s*. Oslo: Fafo.

Dribbusch, H., S. Lehndorff, and T. Schulten. 2017. Two Worlds of Unionism? German Manufacturing and Service Unions Since the Great Recession. In *Rough Waters: European Trade Unions in a Time of Crises*, ed. S. Lehndorff, H. Dribbusch, and T. Schulten, 97–220. Brussels: ETUI.

Erne, R. 2008. *European Unions: Labor's Quest for a Transnational Democracy*. Ithaca: Cornell University Press.

ETUC. 2019. *ETUC Action Program 2019–2023*. Brussels: ETUC.

Furåker, B., and M. Bengtsson. 2013. On the Road to Transnational Cooperation? Results from a Survey among European Trade Unions. *European Journal of Industrial Relations* 19 (2): 161–177.

Furåker, B., and K. Lovén Seldén. 2016. Patterns of Speech Activity at ETUC Executive Committee Meetings, 2005–2012. *European Journal of Industrial Relations* 22 (1): 57–71.

Gajewska, K. 2009. *Transnational Labour Solidarity: Mechanisms of Commitment to Cooperation Within the European Trade Union Movement*. London: Routledge.

Glassner, V., and K. Vandaele. 2012. Which Way Towards Europeanization of Trade Union Strategies? Regional Differences in Trade Union Officers' views. Paper Presented at ILERA World Congress 2012, Philadephia.

Glassner, V., and T. Pusch. 2013. Towards a Europeanization of Wage Bargaining? Evidence from the Metal Sector. *European Journal of Industrial Relations* 19 (2): 145–160.

Gollbach, J., and T. Schulten. 2000. Cross-Border Collective Bargaining Networks in Europe. *European Journal of Industrial Relations* 6 (2): 161–179.

Greenwood, J. 2007. *Interest Representation in the European Union*, 2nd ed. Basingstoke: Palgrave Macmillan.

Gumbrell-McCormick, R., and R. Hyman. 2013. *Trade Unions in Western Europe: Hard Times, Hard Choices*. Oxford: Oxford University Press.

Henning, K. 2015a. Not Dominant but Existent: Involvement of Trade Unions from EU Member States of Eastern Enlargement in European Trade Union Federations. In *Interest Representation and Europeanization of Trade Unions from EU Member States of the Eastern Enlargement*, ed. C. Landgraf and H. Pleines, 73–111. Stuttgart: Ibidem.

Henning, K. 2015b. Trade Unions and Industrial Relations in the EU Member States of Eastern Enlargement. In *Interest Representation and Europeanization of Trade Unions from EU Member States of the Eastern Enlargement*, ed. C. Landgraf and H. Pleines, 53–71. Stuttgart: Ibidem.

Hyman, R. 2001. *Understanding European Trade Unionism: Between Market, Class and Society.* London: Sage.

Hyman, R. 2004. Is Industrial Relations Theory Always Ethnocentric? In *Theoretical Perspectives on Work and the Employment Relationship*, ed. B.E. Kaufman, 265–292. Champaign, IL: Industrial Relations Research Association.

Hyman, R. 2005. Trade Unions and the Politics of the European Social Model. *Economic and Industrial Democracy* 26 (9): 9–40.

Keune, M., and P. Marginson. 2013. Transnational Industrial Relations as Multi-level Governance: Interdependencies in European Social Dialogue. *British Journal of Industrial Relations* 51 (3): 473–497.

Larsson, B. 2012. Obstacles to Transnational Trade Union Cooperation in Europe—Results from a European Survey. *Industrial Relations Journal* 43 (2): 152–170.

Larsson, B. 2014. Transnational Trade Union Action in Europe—The Significance of National and Sectoral Industrial Relations. *European Societies* 16 (3): 378–400.

Larsson, B. 2015. Trade Union Channels for Influencing European Union Policies. *Nordic Journal of Working Life Studies* 5 (3): 101–121.

Larsson, B. 2017. Cultural Borders as Obstacles to European Trade Union Cooperation. In *Cultural Borders and European Integration*, ed. M. Andrén, 53–67. CERGU: Gothenburg.

Larsson, B. 2020. Cultural Obstacles to Trade Union Cooperation in Europe. *Nordic Journal of Working Life Studies* 10 (1): 1–16.

Larsson, B., and A. Törnberg. 2019. Sectoral Networks of Transnational Trade Union Cooperation in Europe. *Economic and Industrial Democracy.* Published online ahead of print. https://doi.org/10.1177/0143831x19853871.

Lehndorff, S., H. Dribbusch, and T. Schulten. 2017. European Trade Unions in a Time of Crises—An Overview. In *Rough Waters: European Trade Unions in a Time of Crises*, ed. S. Lehndorff, H. Dribbusch, and T. Schulten, 7–35. Brussels: ETUI.

Léonard, E., E. Perin, and P. Pochet. 2012. The European Sectoral Social Dialogue as a Tool for Coordination Across Europe? In *The European Union and Industrial Relations: New Procedures, New Context*, ed. S. Smismans, 56–77. Manchester: Manchester University Press.

Lovén Seldén, K. 2014. Laval and Trade Union Cooperation: Views on the Mobilizing Potential of the Case. *International Journal of Comparative Labour Law and Industrial Relations* 30 (1): 87–104.

Magnusson, L., and S. Murhem. 2009. European Integration and Nordic Trade Unions. In *Regional Cooperation and the International Organizations: The Nordic Model in Transnational Alignment*, ed. N. Götz and H. Haggrén, 185–200. Oxon: Routledge.

Marginson, P., and K. Sisson. 2004. *European Integration and Industrial Relations: Multi-level Governance in the Making*. Basingstoke: Palgrave Macmillan.

Müller, T., and H.-W. Platzer. 2017. The European Trade Union Federations: Profiles and Power Resources—Changes and Challenges in Times of Crises. In *Rough Waters: European Trade Unions in a Time of Crises*, ed. S. Lehndorff, H. Dribbusch, and T. Schulten, 303–329. Brussels: ETUI.

Müller, T., H.-W. Platzer, and S. Rüb. 2010. Transnational Company Policy and Coordination of Collective Bargaining—New Challenges and Roles for European Industry Federations. *Transfer: European Review of Labour and Research* 16 (4): 509–524.

Müller, T., H.-W. Platzer, and S. Rüb. 2013. *Transnational Company Agreements and the Role of European Works Councils in Negotiations*. Brussels: ETUI.

Nordin, P. 2009. Membership, Dependencies and Free Riding in Networks—A Case Study of the European Metal Sector. *Industrial Relations and Human Resources Journal* 11 (6): 73–92.

Pernicka, S., and V. Glassner. 2014. Transnational Trade Union Strategies Towards European Wage Policy: A Neo-institutional Framework. *European Journal of Industrial Relations* 20 (4): 317–334.

Prosser, T. 2016. Economic Union without Social Union: The Strange Case of the European Social Dialogue. *Journal of European Social Policy* 26 (5): 460–472.

Rhodes, M. 2015. Employment Policy: Between Efficacy and Experimentation. In *Policy Making in the European Union*, ed. H. Wallace, M.A. Pollack, and A.R. Young, 294–317. Oxford: Oxford University Press.

Seeliger, M. 2019. *Trade Unions in the Course of European Integration: The Social Construction of Organized Interests*. London: Routledge.

Steiert, R. 2009. *Multinationals and Unions. World Company Councils and World Works Councils as Strategies of Union Counter-Force*. IndustriALL Global Union. http://www.industriall-union.org/sites/default/files/migration/imf/RelatedFiles/10030911201810005/2009_RS_WKA_WBR_Gewerkschaften_eng_endg3.pdf.

Traxler, F., and E. Mermet. 2003. Coordination of Collective Bargaining: The Case of Europe. *Transfer: European Review of Labour and Research* 9 (2): 229–246.

Traxler, F., B. Brandl, V. Glassner, and A. Ludwig. 2008. Can Cross-Border Coordination Bargaining Work? *European Journal of Industrial Relations* 14 (2): 217–237.

Visser, J., M. Beentjes, M. van Gerven, and V. Di Stasio. 2009. The Quality of Industrial Relations and the Lisbon Strategy. *Industrial Relations in Europe 2008*, 45–72. Luxembourg: Publications Office of the European Union.

Vulkan, P., and B. Larsson. 2019. Patterns of Transnational Trade Union Cooperation in Europe: The Effects of Regimes, Sectors and Resources. *European Journal of Industrial Relations* 25 (2): 147–162.

Open Access This chapter is licensed under the terms of the Creative Commons Attribution 4.0 International License (http://creativecommons.org/licenses/by/4.0/), which permits use, sharing, adaptation, distribution and reproduction in any medium or format, as long as you give appropriate credit to the original author(s) and the source, provide a link to the Creative Commons license and indicate if changes were made.

The images or other third party material in this chapter are included in the chapter's Creative Commons license, unless indicated otherwise in a credit line to the material. If material is not included in the chapter's Creative Commons license and your intended use is not permitted by statutory regulation or exceeds the permitted use, you will need to obtain permission directly from the copyright holder.

3

The European Trade Union Movement and the Issue of Statutory Minimum Wages

Abstract Most countries in Europe have minimum wage legislation, but there are some exceptions such as the Nordic countries. The issue has clearly divided European trade unions and Nordic unions represent a foothold for the resistance to this kind of regulation. To provide a more detailed picture of European labour organizations' arguments for and against minimum wage legislation, data from interviews and surveys as well as documents are used. There is obviously a deep cleavage within the European trade union movement and the chapter also describes how the ETUC has handled the diverging positions.

Keywords Statutory minimum wages · Trade union disagreement · ETUC compromise

Introduction

We now turn to a topic that has caused a great deal of debate within the European trade union movement: the issue of statutory minimum wages. Most Nordic trade unions as well as some others take a negative view on minimum wage legislation—in sharp contrast to many other organizations in different parts of Europe (e.g., Eldring and Alsos 2012: 84–87;

2015; Furåker 2017; Furåker and Bengtsson 2013: 172–173; Furåker and Lovén Seldén 2013; Schulten 2008: 434; 2014; Schulten et al. 2015: 345–350; Seeliger 2019: 54–61, 155–172; Vande Keybus 2012). Because of these differences of opinion, the issue has been repeatedly debated within the ETUC that has faced difficulties in finding a common policy on the matter. It seems, however, that the issue was settled—at least temporarily—some years ago. The present chapter describes parts of the discussion.

Our purpose is to examine somewhat more closely the arguments for and against statutory minimum wages and how the ETUC has handled the issue. We make use of various kinds of data derived from interviews, surveys and documents. Data were collected in our two research projects described in Chapter 1 of this book. To begin with, we briefly outline some of the characteristics of minimum wage legislation in Europe. Then there is a section on the principal pros and cons of statutory minimum wages, commonly brought forward by trade unions. For the purpose of describing these opinions, interviews with trade union officials are particularly important. After that we report a series of relevant results from our two surveys. Several questions referred to the organizations' attitudes to statutory minimum wages, among other things whether they could see advantages and disadvantages with legislation. Next we turn to the cleavage in the European trade union movement and how the ETUC has managed to reach a compromise. The chapter ends with a concluding discussion.

Statutory Minimum Wages in Europe: A Brief Background

Most EU Member States have legislated minimum wage levels; there are only six exceptions: Austria, Denmark, Cyprus, Finland, Italy and Sweden (Eurofound 2019b). Both Cyprus and Italy appear to be on the road to introduce statutory minima. In Cyprus there is occupation-specific statutory minimum wages for some and collectively agreed minimum wages for others. Austria has had a debate on the issue, but so far kept its system relying on collective agreements. Iceland, Norway and

Switzerland, which are not members in the EU, have no legislation. It should be added that both Iceland and Norway, as well as Finland, admit extension of collective agreements by law, although in the Norwegian case this option has been less often made use of (Eldring and Alsos 2015: 71–78). Denmark and Sweden do not have statutory minimum wages or any *erga omnes* rules. Germany is currently the most recent country to have adopted legislation. This occurred in 2015 through a political decision in spite of some criticism from the social partners (Eurofound 2019b: 2).

There are significant differences among the countries with legislation as to the levels of statutory minimum wages (Eurofound 2019a). Luxembourg has the highest level—nominally more than seven times higher than Bulgaria, which has the lowest. The rough general pattern is that the highest figures appear in North Western European countries and the lowest in the East with the South in between. Most countries have had increases in real terms since 2010, in particular Romania, Bulgaria and Lithuania. In some cases, especially France, Malta and the Netherlands, the increases are small and for Greece and Belgium we actually discover a decrease.

With huge differences in living standards across Europe we could expect to see more or less corresponding cross-national differences in the levels of statutory minimum wages. Therefore the so-called Kaitz index is perhaps a more interesting piece of information. This indicator measures the ratio between the legal minimum wage and the average (mean or median) wage in a country. From the OECD database, we can convey information on the Kaitz index 2017 among EU Member States. In relation to median wages of full-time workers, it was highest for France and Romania (both with 0.62), followed by Portugal (0.61) and the lowest figures turned out for Spain (0.40), the Czech Republic and Estonia (both with 0.41). Measured as a proportion of mean wages for full-time workers, France is still at the top (0.50), ahead of three countries with 0.44: Poland, Romania and the United Kingdom. At the bottom, we find Greece (0.33), Spain (0.34) and the Czech Republic and Estonia (both with 0.35).

Another indicator is the proportion of workers being paid at the level of statutory minimum wages or even lower (Eurofound 2019a: 23–24).

It varies substantially across Europe. Poland has the highest proportion (13.7%), followed by the United Kingdom, Luxembourg, Germany and Portugal with figures above 10%. The lowest proportions appear for the Czech Republic (2%), with Malta, Belgium and Croatia just a little bit higher.

In 12 of the EU Member States, there are special rates for certain categories (Eurofound 2019a: 26). Mostly these special rates apply to younger or less-skilled workers. The goal is to make these workers more attractive in the labour market by letting employers hire them to lower costs than would be the case with the ordinary statutory minimum wages. In some countries, for example Hungary, there are higher rates for skilled employees.

Some recent research in Europe covers the relationship between statutory minimum wages and such aspects as working hours and employment (Eurofound 2019a: 34). We have access to new studies on these topics in Germany, Greece and Ireland (Bonin et al. 2019; Bruttel 2019; Caliendo et al. 2018; Georgiadis et al. 2018; McGuiness and Redmond 2018). The general result is that the impact on employment has been small. Legislation has led to an increase in hourly wages, but it has also tended to reduce working hours. When Ireland increased the minimum wage level with 6% in 2016, it led to a substantial decline of working hours, especially for those with temporary employment contracts (McGuiness and Redmond 2018).

An interesting case is Germany that implemented minimum wages legislation in 2015. With a high level of minimum pay, the new regulation apparently has favoured 'low educated, marginally employed, women and people with migration background' (Caliendo et al. 2018: 30). At the same time, overall employment appeared to have undergone a slight decrease, due to diminished recruitment and a decrease of marginal employment, that is, so-called mini-jobs. No clear effects were found on people's livelihood, because there was also a clear reduction in working hours. Poverty and inequality were therefore not much affected. Finally, available evidence pointed to a significant non-compliance with the rules; large numbers of employees were paid less than required by law.

Another German study found rather similar results (Bonin et al. 2019). After two years there had been a reduction of marginal employment, but the researchers could not confirm any significant changes in regular employment and unemployment. One factor that should not be neglected is that people who previously had mini-jobs to some extent had become self-employed and therefore stood outside the minimum wage legislation.

A third study also found that the increase of hourly wages did not imply higher monthly pay, as there was a parallel reduction of working hours (Bruttel 2019). Companies that paid less than the minimum wage level before 2015 increased their prices, but nonetheless got lower profits. However, the effects of the legislation on the overall economy appeared to have been limited. Furthermore, the problem of non-compliance was again emphasized; it remained a crucial task to ensure better compliance. Yet another conclusion was that people's welfare dependency and risk for poverty did not diminish.

An interesting question is whether the bottom level is set sufficiently high to avoid poverty. The statutory minimum wages in many European countries are so low that they do not prevent income poverty (Schulten 2014: 13). It should be noted that the percentage of working poor is generally lower in the Nordic countries as well as in Italy than elsewhere in Europe (Eldring and Alsos 2015: 34–36; Schulten 2014). As a consequence, it may not be so easy to convince trade unions in these countries that legislation is necessary to avoid in-work poverty.

Arguments for Legislated Minimum Wages

Trade unions can have different motives for taking a certain position in the debate on statutory minimum wages. It is unclear to what extent empirical studies in the field have an impact on the debate. Unions' motives may be more or less ideological or pragmatic and they can show more or less solidarity with various actors. In this and the next section we identify some of the most important arguments among trade unionists for and against minimum wage legislation. Indicators of these claims are also included in one of the empirical datasets (survey 2) that we use. We start with arguments about possible advantages.

Legislated minimum wages might secure that all workers—and not only the organized—are covered (Furåker and Lovén Seldén 2013; Schulten 2008; Schulten and Watt 2007). In one of our studies, a Spanish trade union official, interviewed in 2012, presented the argument in the following way (Furåker 2017):

> The strongest argument for minimum wages is that it is necessary to protect all workers by one instrument… But it is not necessary to have it by law; it could just as well be by collective bargaining. This is a difference of culture, because in some other countries it is a tradition to protect only affiliates—perhaps 10, 20, 30%—and not workers who are not members. We come from a tradition in which the unions fight for all. In Spain we have 19-20% union density and 80% are non-members.

The assumption was then that employers comply with the minimum wage legislation. It is worth being repeated that studies of the German introduction of such legislation emphasized that there could be some substantial non-compliance (Bruttel 2019: 11–12; Caliendo et al. 2018: 30). Yet we can expect that even if not all unorganized employees are protected by law, some of them are likely to be. It can still be a fairly effective method of creating protection for the unorganized.

One thing to note is that the Spanish union official did not declare that legislation would be the only option; his opinion was that minimum wages could just as well be decided through collective bargaining. The point is, though, that if merely very few of the workers are unionized, a majority may not be protected by collective bargaining—unless there is extension of collective agreements by law.

Two German trade union representatives who were interviewed together said that they would prefer wages be set through collective bargaining, but if this was not feasible, other solutions must come in (Furåker and Lovén Seldén 2013: 514). What they actually referred to was minimum wage legislation. This should be seen in light of the declining union density rate in Germany like in many other countries, implying that more and more employees stayed unorganized.

Another Spanish union official, who was interviewed in 2012, also stressed how important it would be with minimum wage legislation to protect workers, but he brought up yet another principal argument by pointing out that minimum wage legislation establishes a clear limit to wage dumping (Furåker and Lovén Seldén 2013: 514): 'The second reason may be that if you have a minimum wage you have a limit to wage dumping'.

This argument was also mentioned in several other interviews that we conducted in our two research projects (cf. Vande Keybus 2012). Again, a crucial problem is whether employers comply with the legislation, because non-compliance can be interpreted as just another expression for wage dumping. It is at least likely that statutory minima establish some limits to dumping of that kind. Therefore, they might be seen as measures to decrease inequalities in society (Schulten 2008; Schulten and Watt 2007; Vande Keybus 2012).

A mechanism that helps prevent wage dumping may also contribute to decreasing poverty. The German studies referred to above (Bruttel 2019; Caliendo et al. 2018) did not find this kind of effect, but the poverty-reducing impact of statutory minimum wages has still often been brought forward as a positive argument in the debate. Sometimes it has been proposed that minimum wage legislation should help people get a 'living wage' (Schulten 2008; Schulten et al. 2015: 339–341).

We should keep a distinction between minimum wage legislation at national level and such regulation at European level. National legislation already exists in many countries, but could be extended to countries without legislation. It is also possible to make rules stricter and more difficult not to follow. In addition, there is the question about the minimum wage levels in relation to the general wage situation in a country. At European level, no regulation of minimum wages exists, but it might be implemented in different ways. There are many advocates for introducing a common European policy in this regard (Eldring and Alsos 2015: 13–21; Fernández-Marcías and Vacas-Soriano 2016; Schulten 2008, 2014; Schulten and Müller 2014; Vande Keybus 2012; Vaughan-Whitehead 2010). This is a more far-reaching idea, which might be especially difficult to accept for unions with a negative attitude even to national legislation. It is of course unrealistic with a single minimum wage level throughout the EU. What is closest at hand would be to implement an EU directive according to which statutory minimum wages should be set at, for example, 60% of the average wage in each Member State (cf. Schulten 2014). In the following, both of these dimensions will be touched upon. First, we proceed to describe possible arguments against minimum wage legislation, with primarily a national-level focus.

Arguments against Legislated Minimum Wages

From previous research and various documents, we can outline the main arguments behind trade unions' negative views on statutory minimum wages. On the whole, the countries without statutory minimum wages appear to have a viable option. The Nordic countries have high union density rates and a high degree of collective bargaining coverage, although there is some variation between them. This is true even though union density tends to fall everywhere in the Nordic region except Iceland. Other countries without minimum wage legislation have lower density rates and lower levels of collective bargaining coverage, but compared to many other countries they still score relatively high in these respects.

Legislation on minimum wages is regarded as a restriction on the partners' freedom to conclude independent agreements (Eldring and Alsos 2015: 85). When we interviewed highly placed officials in the Swedish trade union confederations some years ago, the principle of independent collective bargaining was energetically stressed as being very important. Such an opinion was communicated very distinctly in an interview with a Swedish trade union official (Furåker and Lovén Seldén 2013: 514).

> The main argument against [a minimum wage policy] is that it contradicts our strategy of organizing, negotiating and signing collective agreements and monitoring whether the collective agreements are respected, and by doing so taking control over the destiny of workers… To act as a

supply cartel is simply... a fundamental traditional trade union view. To support a statutory minimum wage is a strong violation of that tradition.

Moreover, it seems that the Nordic trade unions are also afraid that an acceptance of minimum wage legislation would be followed by further European regulations (Eldring and Alsos 2015: 84). They simply want to safeguard the Nordic model with its emphasis on the autonomy and integrity of collective bargaining.

We may ask whether or not collective bargaining leads to better results for workers. Minimum wage legislation should at least maintain a lowest limit, unless employers fail to comply with the law. A relevant piece of information in this context is brought up by Line Eldring and Kristin Alsos (2015: 74–78, 85); they make the observation that, in selected key industries in the Nordic countries, wages significantly exceeded the agreed minima. This outcome applied also in industries with low collective bargaining coverage. The explanation is held to be a contagion effect of collective agreements. Legislated minimum wages can then be a blow in the air and this is not all: their consequences may even go in the opposite direction. Actually, it is a possible disadvantage recognized by some of those arguing for legislation as well. One of our interviewees, from a Belgian trade union, pointed out that because legislation would set the lowest pay level, it could be difficult to obtain a higher wage than that (Furåker and Lovén Seldén 2013: 515). The same opinion was expressed in another interview with a Spanish union official (Furåker and Lovén Seldén 2013: 515):

> Once you have a minimum wage, sometimes it can be very difficult to improve a lot on that minimum wage. So you have your minimum wage and that is okay, but [it] can be difficult to have improvements on that because that is the economic reality... and I suppose that would be the main reason against it.

It should be noted that the Belgian and the Spanish unionists just mentioned were both strongly in favour of legislation. A further possible disadvantage with state regulation of minimum wages is that it could weaken employees' motivation to become unionized (Eldring and Alsos

2015: 85–86; Furåker and Lovén Seldén 2013: 515). It is always a critical issue for trade unions to recruit members, and this will certainly not be made simpler if wages are set without unions having very much to say. This reasoning could be relevant in relation to employer organizations too. However, unions (and employers' associations) may have a role in contributing to deciding the legislated minimum wages. Thus, unions could get a more visible role at societal level, even if this would be restricted to peak-level organizations (Furåker and Lovén Seldén 2013: 515; Vande Keybus 2012).

In the last two sections, we have brought up a number of possible advantages and disadvantages of statutory minimum wages. The ambition has not been to provide an exhaustive description, but we have tried to focus on rather tangible aspects. There are other aspects that could also be mentioned, for example, that a joint position among trade unions on European minimum wage legislation could have an important symbolic value, 'giving substance to Social Europe' (Vaughan-Whitehead 2010: 529).

What Do Survey Data Tell Us?

In our two surveys, we have some questions concerning statutory minimum wages. As to the 2010–2011 survey we limit the presentation to countries in which the number of responding unions exceeded 10, which means results for 11 countries. The questionnaire included a number of items intended to gauge attitudes to minimum wages. Respondents were asked to what extent they agreed with certain statements—to a high degree, to some degree, to a low degree[1] or not at all.

The first statement says that it would require EU legislation on minimum wages to prevent wage dumping. The second item taps the desirability of future developments of national legislation on minimum wages, either through the introduction of such legislation (if it does not exist) or through stricter legislation (if it already exists). Union representatives were accordingly expected to interpret the statement in accordance with their own location. The third item in the questionnaire deals with the issue whether, at transnational level, it would be desirable in the future with European legislation on minimum wages.

Table 3.1 presents the summary indicators for the 11 countries on each of the items. Summary indicators are calculated in the same way as in two of the tables in Chapter 2 (Tables 2.1 and 2.3). Starting with the first statement, we should note that at this time not only the four Nordic countries were without minimum wage legislation; this was also the case for Germany. It is striking that all the responding unions in Belgium, Poland and Spain agreed at least to some degree that it would take EU legislation on minimum pay to prevent wage dumping. The summary indicators for France and Germany are slightly lower because some unions deviate from the common pattern. Still, in both cases a clear majority of unions expressed a great deal of agreement with the statement. The United Kingdom comes next in the ranking with a lower level of agreement, but still with a markedly positive score after the summary indicator calculation. Finland also gets a positive end result, but it is not very far from zero. For the remaining Nordic countries, Denmark, Norway and Sweden, the summary indicators are negative. Denmark is not so distant from Finland, while Sweden is undoubtedly farthest away.

The response pattern on the second item is fairly similar to the first one, but there are some differences. Instead of Belgium, Poland and Spain at the top, we find Germany, Poland and Spain. We can add that 90% of the 20 Polish respondents agreed 'to a high degree' (not shown), implying that they would like to have stricter legislation. For Spain, the result goes in the same direction, but with a much lower proportion answering 'to a high degree'. As to Germany, the outcome suggests that national legislation on minimum wages was, more or less, on the unions' wish list. In Belgium, three out of eleven trade unions did not select the two most positive response options and this was the case for five out of eighteen French organizations as well. Hence, the summary indicators in the two countries are quite similar. An interpretation of this is that many respondents were fairly satisfied with the national minimum wage legislation; they did not find it desirable to make it stricter. The British unions emerge as more divided. For the Nordic cluster, we see strongly negative figures in the summary indicator column. Notably, the proportions

Table 3.1 Summary indicators on attitudes to minimum wage issues

	To prevent wage dumping, EU legislation on minimum wages is required		For the future, on national level, to what degree does your organization find it desirable with regulation/stricter regulation by legislation on minimum wages?		For the future, on transnational level, to what degree does your organization find it desirable with European legislation on minimum wages?		
	Summary indicators	Do not know	Summary indicators	Do not know	Summary indicators	Do not know	n
Belgium	100	0	55	9	91	0	11
Poland	100	0	100	0	95	0	20
Spain	100	0	100	0	93	0	14
France	88	6	50	6	78	11	18
Germany	88	0	100	0	81	0	16
UK	58	11	6	0	-17	17	17–19
Finland	6	6	-67	7	-69	6	15–16
Denmark	-5	5	-70	0	-74	5	20
Norway	-25	8	-54	13	-78	4	23–24
Sweden	-42	8	-78	0	-81	3	37–39

Source Own data, survey 1

answering that they did not agree at all are particularly high in Sweden and Denmark.

The final item in Table 3.1 deals with the issue whether it would be desirable in the future with European legislation on minimum wages. The highest summary indicators—for Poland, Spain and Belgium—are then slightly below 100, as a few trade unions in these countries expressed doubts about such an arrangement. German and French respondents also appear with high positive figures. The British unions have a negative summary indicator, although far from the Nordic unions, which all show very little consensus on the idea of future European legislation.

With respect to our 2015–2016 survey we have answers from 221 trade unions. The survey contained seven questions with relevance for the minimum wage issue or—to be more specific—statements on which respondents were asked to express their organizations' view. The overriding question was: 'To what degree does your organization agree with the following statements on nationally legislated minimum wages?' Six of the items include statements that can be regarded as arguments for or against national legislation. They gauge whether statutory minimum wages (a) 'are necessary to prevent wage dumping'; (b) 'undermine the role of trade unions'; (c) 'are the best way for unorganized workers to get decent wages'; (d) 'are necessary to prevent poverty'; (e) 'make it more difficult for unions to recruit members' and (f) 'may lead to lower collectively agree wages'. The seventh statement was aimed at exploring attitudes to a possible role for the ETUC and has the following wording: 'ETUC should work for common European norms on minimum wages'. Each of the seven items could be answered in the same way as reported for the items in Table 3.1.

Three of the statements thus represent possible advantages with statutory minimum wages and three others represent possible disadvantages. In the following, we divide the trade unions into three categories. One consists of those in countries with legislated minimum wages and then we have two categories in countries without such legislation: non-Nordic and Nordic. The reason why we treat the Nordic unions separately is that they are frequently depicted as the most negative to political regulation of wage setting (e.g., Furåker 2017; Eldring and Alsos 2012, 2015; Schulten et al. 2015; Seeliger 2019: 155–172). As a consequence, we have only 17 respondents from unions in other countries without legislation, but without this distinction certain interesting differences would not become visible. Table 3.2 gives the responses on the first set of statements, dealing with conceivable advantages with legislation.

As we can see, unions in countries with minimum wage legislation were much more inclined to endorse the statements that contain the arguments in support of such arrangements. This comes out clearly, when we concentrate on the summary indicators. They are strongly positive for unions in countries with statutory minimum wages, but there are some differences between the items: a very high score for the statement regarding wage dumping, distinctly lower on the item regarding the consequences for unorganized workers and somewhere in between for the avoid-poverty statement. There are of course unions, which have expressed a deviant opinion, but they are not that many. For trade unions in non-Nordic countries without statutory minimum wages, the corresponding scores are all much lower, but two out of three are still positive. The exception with a low negative number is the item on legislation as the best way for unorganized workers to get decent wages. In contrast, we find large negative figures for the Nordic trade unions, roughly varying between minus one-third and minus 40 on the summary indicators in the three cases.

Table 3.3 presents the response patterns regarding arguments against statutory minimum wages. In these cases, trade unions in the countries with minimum wage legislation have strongly negative summary indicators. With some variation, this holds for all three items in the table. It seems that these respondents did not generally believe that legislation would undermine the role of unions nor make it more difficult for them to recruit members or that it would lead to lower collectively agreed wages. Again, there are organizations that have responded differently, but very few answered that they agreed 'to a high degree' with these negative statements.

For the unions in non-Nordic countries without legislation, a somewhat different pattern comes out. These organizations have two rather low, but still positive summary indicators: on the first and on the third

Table 3.2 Degree of agreement with various statements on possible advantages of statutory minimum wages. Percentages

	Summary indicators[a]	To a high degree	To some degree	To a low degree	Not at all	Do not know	Total (n)
They prevent wage dumping							
In countries with MWL	81	69	22	8	2	0	100 (125)
In countries without MWL							
- non-Nordic	18	47	12	29	38	0	100 (17)
- Nordic	−40	17	10	23	44	6	100 (70)
They are the best way for unorganized workers to get decent wages							
In countries with MWL	32	27	38	18	15	2	100 (121)
In countries without MWL							
- non-Nordic	−5	24	18	41	6	0	100 (17)
- Nordic	−36	7	20	27	36	10	100 (70)
They are necessary to avoid poverty							
In countries with MWL	68	48	36	12	4	0	100 (122)
In countries without MWL							
- non-Nordic	18	35	24	35	6	0	100 (17)
- Nordic	−34	14	16	24	40	6	100 (70)

[a]Summary indicator = (To a high degree + To some degree) − (To a low degree + Not at all)

Note MWL is an abbreviation for minimum wage legislation

Source Own data, survey 2

Table 3.3 Degree of agreement with various statements on possible disadvantages of statutory minimum wages. Percentages

	Summary indicators[a]	To a high degree	To some degree	To a low degree	Not at all	Do not know	Total (n)
They undermine the role of trade unions							
In countries with MWL	−67	4	11	23	59	3	100 (119)
In countries without MWL							
– non-Nordic	6	29	24	12	35	0	100 (17)
– Nordic	34	28	36	10	20	6	100 (69)
They make it more difficult for unions to recruit members							
In countries with MWL	−54	5	17	30	46	2	100 (123)
In countries without MWL							
– non-Nordic	−40	6	24	29	41	0	100 (17)
– Nordic	−8	14	24	17	29	16	100 (70)
They may lead to lower collectively agreed wages							
In countries with MWL	−45	8	18	28	43	3	100 (119)
In countries without MWL							
– non-Nordic	17	29	29	12	29	0	100 (17)
– Nordic	42	27	37	11	11	13	100 (70)

[a]Summary indicator = (To a high degree + To some degree) − (To a low degree + Not at all)

Note MWL is an abbreviation for minimum wage legislation

Source Own data, survey 2

Table 3.4 Degree of agreement with the statement 'ETUC should work for common European norms on minimum wages'. Percentages

	Summary indicators[a]	To a high degree	To some degree	To a low degree	Not at all	Do not know	Total (n)
In countries with MWL	**84**	63	28	7	0	2	100 (123)
In countries without MWL							
– non-Nordic	**64**	35	47	18	0	0	100 (17)
– Nordic	**–38**	11	13	19	43	14	100 (70)

[a]Summary indicator = (To a high degree + To some degree) - (To a low degree + Not at all)
Note MWL is an abbreviation for minimum wage legislation
Source Own data, survey 2

statement. For them, the second item is an exception with a highly negative balance, not so far from what we see for unions in countries with statutory minimum wages. The Nordic unions also get a negative summary indicator on this statement, even if it is much closer to zero. In other words, most of the responding organizations did not find that legislation would make it more difficult for them to recruit members. With respect to the first and the third item, the Nordic unions generally agreed to a high or some degree with the presumed disadvantages. We could note that the proportions of 'do-not-know' answers are especially high in the Nordic cluster. Although partly with lower numbers, this also applies to Table 3.2.

On the seventh item in the questionnaire—on whether the ETUC should work for common minimum wage norms in Europe—most trade unions in countries with legislation responded in the affirmative, as we can see in Table 3.4. There is not much doubt on the topic among these organizations; most of them at least appeared to be sure about one thing to which the ETUC should devote its power.

The non-Nordic unions in countries without legislation also tended to agree with the statement, although the summary indicator is somewhat lower. In contrast, the Nordic respondents provided a very different set of answers, adding up to a distinctly negative summary value, but 14% replied that they did not know.

The Cleavage in the European Trade Union Movement

Our examination of data points to a distinct conclusion. While many unions in Europe are strongly in favour of minimum wage legislation, others and especially Nordic unions are very negative to it (Eldring and Alsos 2015; Furåker and Lovén Seldén 2013; Furåker 2017; Schulten et al. 2015; Seeliger 2019: 155–172). Typically, in the Nordic countries this kind of arrangement is at best considered to be 'a necessary evil' (Eldring and Alsos 2015). In other words, there are rival views on the topic in the European trade union movement. The Nordic trade unions may seem to be united in their resistance to minimum wage legislation, but we should note some cracks in the facade. Also in this region we find some differences of opinion and some disagreement. As the summary indicators presented above are never 100 or −100 for the Nordic unions, some of them must have responded in another way than the majority. Moreover, the proportions of 'do-not-know' answers turned out to be highest in the Nordic cluster. Anyway, some Nordic unions were evidently not very negative to legislation or could not take a stand.

A much talked about event took place in 2014 in Copenhagen, where the ETUC Executive Committee held a meeting. Bente Sorgenfrey, Chairperson of the Confederation of Professionals in Demark, President for the Council of Nordic Trade Unions and member of the ETUC Executive Committee, then spoke in favour of statutory minimum wages (Eurofound 2015). After bringing up her arguments at a press conference there was an immediate and massive reaction from both other Danish unions and Danish employers' associations, which all emphatically said no thanks to minimum wage legislation. This was not the only time that Sorgenfrey was in focus. *Nordic Labour Journal* (2015: 3–7) had a thematic issue on statutory minimum wages and there she was quoted, highlighting that many European colleagues advocated European minimum wage legislation and arguing that Nordic trade union leaders should support them. She was also reported to mention that the Norwegian model with the possibility of extending collective agreements by law could be a reasonable way forward.

Another example of differing Nordic opinions stems from the Swedish Transport Workers' Union. This organization raised the issue of making collective agreements into law (*Nordic Labour Journal* 2015: 14–15) at about the same time as Sorgenfrey came out with her views on the delicate question. In an interview, conducted within our second research project in 2015, the chairman of the organized transport workers noted that this initiative was 'not popular in the LO^2', in spite of his argument 'that we are in the industry that has been most exposed to social dumping'—which, he said, would require some action.

Albeit these examples, a Nordic comparison showed that the Danish and Swedish trade unions were the most negative to minimum wage legislation (Furåker 2017). The analysis also revealed that larger organizations were less prone to see advantages with legislation and large organizations are of course relatively influential in the cooperation within the ETUC.

It should not be very surprising that unions in countries where statutory minimum wages exist are more likely to see advantages with legislation than are unions in countries without such measures. Obviously, the reverse also applies. The most important observation is, however, that the diverging opinions create conflicts in connection with transnational trade union cooperation. The continuing resistance to state regulation among Nordic trade unions makes us quote three other researchers asking why 'the apparently robust and sustainable Nordic labour market regimes could feel threatened by a European minimum wage policy that is intended primarily for countries with low minimum wage levels or no functioning minimum wage regimes' (Schulten et al. 2015: 350). The answer is most likely a fear among the Nordic unions that their own model would be negatively affected by legislation and that acceptance of it might be the first step towards further European regulations (Eldring and Alsos 2015: 84).

We may also ask whether the concept of solidarity is relevant. Rebecka Gumbrell-McCormick and Richard Hyman (2015; Hyman 2002) have shown that this concept can be interpreted in different ways. Among other things, the point of departure for trade unions is that workers' interests need to be taken care of by a collective organization. There is also a distinction between solidarity *with* and solidarity *against* (Gumbrell-McCormick and Hyman 2015: 2). A typical example can be when workers feel solidarity *with* one another and *against* employers. As to the European discussion on statutory minimum wages, it seems that we find trade unions standing against each other. Whereas some organizations want to campaign for stricter national legislation, more generous minimum wage levels and perhaps a common European policy on the issue, others are simply against any such attempt. It is likely that both camps are fighting for those they feel solidarity with. The basis for the cleavage in the European trade union movement is the differences in organizational, structural and institutional power that exist between unions in different parts of Europe (cf. Chapter 1; Gumbrell-McCormick and Hyman 2013: 30–31; Lehndorff et al. 2017).

Not least within the ETUC, we see these conflicting views colouring the debates over the years. Martin Seeliger (2019: 155–172) gives a vivid portrayal of the intense disagreements among European trade unionists on the issue of statutory minimum wages. Among other things, he interviewed a number of Hungarian, Polish and Swedish trade union representatives and these interview data are used as empirical evidence in his analysis. The Poles and the Hungarians were positive to minimum wage legislation and the Swedes were fervently against it. There were occasions when the debate was very heated, apparently with more solidarity against than solidarity with unions in other countries.

This also points at how important labour market policies and regulations are for transnational trade union cooperation. As shown in Chapter 2, differences in these respects were judged to be the second most important obstacle to such collaboration and similarities were considered the most important facilitator. It has simply been difficult to find a common cooperative basis for unions with respect to the issue of minimum wage legislation.

The ETUC is what Göran Ahrne and Nils Brunsson (2008) call a meta-organization, with other organizations as members (cf. also Lovén Seldén 2014: 30–31). One characteristic of meta-organizations is their tendency to search for consensus in decision-making (Ahrne and Brunsson 2008: 123–124). It is of great importance for building up legitimacy in relation to their members. We can see that the ETUC has handled disagreement regarding the issue of statutory minimum wages in line with this observation.

The minimum wage issue was on the agenda at the ETUC Congress in Seville in 2007. In a strategy and action plan, it was suggested, among other things, that the organization and its affiliated unions should work for the following (ETUC 2007: 138):

- Support union campaigns for effective minimum wages in those countries where the unions consider them necessary. Targets should be set as part of a purposeful campaign towards "living" wages and to tackle the growing gaps between rich and poor, men and women.

- Targets to close the pay gaps should also be adopted by those unions whose confidence in the effectiveness of their collective bargaining processes means that they do not need legally established minimum wages.
- Explore continually the scope for united campaigns at European level, led by the ETUC, for common standards on minimum pay and income, and for collective bargaining strategies. Currently it may be that, for example, the differences in skills, productivity, living standards and union policies are too great for a campaign on common European-wide minimum wage mechanisms, but as circumstances change the ETUC must be ready to lead a debate on united campaigns.

We can notice that the ETUC balanced the disagreements within the organization. The idea is to support campaigns for minimum wage legislation only 'where unions consider them necessary'. Still, it was considered important to attack pay gaps also in countries where unions did not see a need for minimum wage legislation. In addition to this, it was argued that cross-national differences may be too great for 'a campaign on common European-wide minimum wage mechanisms', although things might change.

After the preparatory phase of the ETUC Congress in Athens 2011, there was a great deal of debate in the organization on minimum wages. It was important for the ETUC to avoid open conflict and the organization therefore needed to find a balance between different interests. In a previous article we compared various documents, showing certain changes of wordings (Furåker and Lovén Seldén 2013: 517, Note 6): In October 2011 the ETUC (2011a: 6) claimed that 'a minimum wage norm would be agreed determining the minimum pay level in each country', but only somewhat later, in December 2011, the organization stated 'that wherever it exists the effective national minimum wage should be at least equal to 50 per cent of the average wage or 60 per cent of the median wage' (ETUC 2011b: 6). The key words are 'in each country' and 'where it exists' and the latter wording is a remission to those who did not want legislation (Furåker and Lovén Seldén 2013: 517, Note 6).

A stringent formulation of the ETUC position on statutory minimum wages, which also strikes the balance between the diverging interests came some years later (ETUC 2012a; cf. also 2013):

> Wage setting [is] to remain a national matter and be dealt with according to national practices and industrial relations systems. Negotiations between social partners at the relevant level are the best tool to secure good wages and working conditions. The statutory minimum wage in those countries where trade unions consider it necessary should be increased substantially. In any event all wage floors should respect Council of Europe standards on fair wages.

The main idea in the above quotation is that national industrial relations systems and practices should have a crucial role in wage setting. The ETUC speaks in favour of collective bargaining as the best method of obtaining adequate wages and working conditions, but trade unions cannot always achieve their goals in that way. If that is the case, there is no other possibility but to rely on legislation. This is obviously the most relevant option for many European unions. What the ETUC did was to recognize that different solutions should apply in different national contexts.

Somewhat later, in the *Paris Manifesto*, the organization expressed the following opinion (ETUC 2015b: 8):

> The autonomy of the social partners at national and European level must be respected. We reject interference by public authorities in social dialogue, collective bargaining or existing collective agreements. Industrial relations should be strengthened and collective agreements extended to cover as many workers as possible, with support for trade union coordination of collective bargaining.

This might even sound like a condemnation of all kinds of state intervention in the relationship between employers and trade unions, but there is also another paragraph (before the one quoted) in the same document, telling something else (ETUC 2015b: 8):

> Statutory minimum wages, where trade unions want them, should be set with the involvement of social partners. The level of a statutory minimum wage should aim for better standards, as advocated by international organisations. This, together with collective bargaining, will help to combat in-work poverty, social and wage dumping, and will foster internal demand. In this context, it is advisable to start discussions on a common reference for national statutory minimum wages, applicable in countries where trade unions want them.

Another aspect is that the ETUC does not believe that statutory minimum wages are sufficient to deal with labour-cost competition and in-work poverty. This is clearly expressed in the action program of 2015 (ETUC 2015a: 33):

> Minimum wages alone cannot offer an adequate response to labour-cost competition and in-work poverty. Strengthening collective bargaining systems and their coverage is essential to prevent a downward slide in wage.

It is also recognized that it has been difficult to establish robust collective bargaining institutions in Central/Eastern Europe. Therefore, '/i/n these countries, minimum wages play a more important role than in others where well-established industrial relations systems are able to secure the best deal for workers'; in other words, 'a balanced and differentiated approach to minimum wages is needed, respecting national practices and needs' (ETUC 2015a: 33).

One important question is where to set the level of statutory minimum wages relative to other wages in a country. As pointed out above, in December 2011, just before the Copenhagen Winter School in February 2012, Copenhagen, the ETUC stated that the 'national minimum wage should be at least equal to 50 per cent of the average wage or 60 per cent of the median wage' (ETUC 2011b: 6). There was also an idea of an ETUC campaign on this topic, but it appears to have been delayed (Seeliger 2019: 56–57, 61, 163). A more recent ETUC (2018) resolution on coordination of collective bargaining and wage policies continues on the same path as before.

The Nordic trade unions have obviously been able to influence the ETUC's position on statutory minimum wages. One important factor behind this is the Council of Nordic Trade Unions. It has separate gatherings to make preparations for ETUC meetings (Seeliger 2019: 169–170, 212–213, 226). The participating organizations' discussions aim to find common positions on various issues and once they are united, they have been very successful in speaking with one voice. Attempts of such coordination in other regions have been less effective. When the Nordic subdivision has agreed on a certain position it is difficult for the ETUC not to take that very seriously.

Conclusion

The general picture in the above analysis is that Nordic trade unions as well as some others are sceptical, not to say absolutely against, of statutory minimum wages. This resistance exists in countries without minimum wage legislation, while the most affirmative attitudes are found in nations with such an arrangement. The majority of the unions in our surveys are located in the latter countries. Typically, they emerge as positive both on the more general questions and on the more specific items on advantages/disadvantages regarding statutory minimum wages. These respondents were mostly confident of claims that legislation is the best method for unorganized workers to obtain decent wages, that it can impede wage dumping and that it is a necessary arrangement to prevent poverty. The opposing unions did not agree very much on these statements. Instead, they were more susceptible to the potential drawbacks of minimum wage legislation. They tended to think that it undermines the role of trade unions and that it may lead to lower collectively agreed wages. A somewhat different outcome showed up on the issue of whether legislated minimum wages would have a negative impact on unions' possibilities of recruiting members. Some responding organizations agreed with this, but still more concurred only to a low degree or not at all. This goes for all the unions in our dataset, but the negative summary indicator for the Nordic unions is much closer to zero than for the other two categories in our analysis.

Another result is that the three categories of unions distinguished also differed with respect to the issue whether the ETUC should work for common European norms on minimum wages. These results are more or less in line with expectations. The Nordic unions were most negative, whereas the other two categories were basically positive, although unions in countries with statutory minimum wages were so to a greater extent. A similar pattern emerged on a couple of items dealing with EU minimum wage legislation in our first survey, but in this case the number of countries and responding unions was much smaller.

Our data indicate that the strongest opposition to minimum wage legislation comes from Nordic trade unions. Denmark, Finland, Iceland, Norway and Sweden undoubtedly show some significant similarities making them special compared with other countries, but there are also differences among them, for example, as mentioned previously, in regard of the possibility of extending collective agreements by law. A principal characteristic is that the Nordic countries have well-developed collective bargaining systems with strong social partners. One indicator of this is union density, which is high in international comparison. In 2017, Iceland had the highest level with over 90% organized (Visser 2019). The corresponding figures in Denmark, Finland and Sweden were a bit below 70%. In Norway, union density was around 52%, still much above what we find in most other countries.

The Nordic bargaining system also has high proportions of employees covered by collective bargaining agreements. After adjustments for certain sectors and occupations excluded from the right to bargain, we again encounter quite high figures: for 2017, 93% in Finland, 89% in Iceland and Sweden, 84% in Denmark and 67% in Norway (Visser 2019). Once more, the Norwegian figure is lower, but it is much higher than for union density in the country. All five Nordic countries have been shown to be above the OECD average in terms of collective bargaining coverage (OECD 2014: 103).

Hence, there are good reasons to distinguish a Nordic model of labour markets and industrial relations (Chapter 1 in this book; Dølvik 2013; Ferner and Hyman 1998; Larsson et al. 2012; Traxler et al. 2001; Visser et al. 2009). The literature also distinguishes four other industrial relations regimes, but it is not obvious that this classification can contribute to the analysis of trade union attitudes to statutory minimum wages.

The divergent opinions within the European trade union movement have been associated with a great deal of debate. For the ETUC it was necessary to arrive at a settlement on minimum wages according to which it is recognized that different solutions are relevant due to national traditions and circumstances. The organization has even emphasized that collective agreements represent the best way to obtain good wages and appropriate working conditions, but that legislation can be necessary elsewhere (ETUC 2012a, b, 2013, 2015a, b). Most Nordic trade unions ought to be quite satisfied with the current ETUC compromise, because its main content is that wage setting should be adjusted to the national context. They have been able to achieve what they wanted to achieve. One reason behind this accomplishment is that the Council of Nordic Trade Unions is an effective sub-organization within the ETUC; it regularly acts unanimously and it is well-prepared for ETUC meetings (Seeliger 2019: 169–170, 226). It should be repeated that Nordic trade unions are characterized by having considerable organizational, structural and institutional power (cf. Chapter 1; Gumbrell-McCormick and Hyman 2013: 30–31; Lehndorff et al. 2017). As long as the ETUC compromise is valid, trade union cooperation in Europe does not have to be negatively affected, although it means that the struggle for legislated minimum wages is not a joint effort of European unions.

It seems that the classification into industrial relations regimes presented in Chapter 1 is of limited value when we examine trade unions' views on statutory minimum wages. The Nordic countries represent one of the five different regimes and in that sense the regime concept is relevant. Including the other four categories does not add much—if anything at all—to the analysis. The cleavage within the European trade union movement is above all a matter of the gap between the Nordic unions with their strong organizations and robust collective bargaining systems and the rest. Hand in hand with this we find lower levels of inequality and relatively high standards of living in the Nordic region. The German unions were for a long time rather strong—although not as strong as the Nordic—but their position was undermined by member and power losses and it was then time for another attitude to and interpretation of the need for minimum wage legislation.

As mentioned previously, solidarity is a concept that can refer to very different phenomena (Gumbrell-McCormick and Hyman 2001; Hyman 2002). Obviously, the unions that are against minimum wage legislation focus on what they see as the best for employees in their own country/countries. It is with them they feel solidarity. The unions that are in favour of legislation do the same, but they have another country or other countries in mind. The positive and the negative side more or less stand against each other, as they feel that the counterpart can negatively impact on what they have. It has evidently been difficult to bridge the gap between the two. The ETUC compromise currently appears to be the only way to handle the cleavage in the European trade union movement.

At present, there is no indication that the Nordic countries would be about to introduce statutory minimum wages. One reason for this is that the key trade unions for the most part have a very negative attitude. It has also been shown that the organizations just below the confederate level are similarly negative (Furåker 2017). The crucial question is however what will happen in the long run. There are constantly new initiatives in Europe to introduce statutory minimum wages. The *Laval* verdict by the European Court of Justice some years ago implies certain drawbacks of not having legislated minima (e.g., Skedinger 2008: 28–29; Woolfson et al. 2010). Without this kind of regulation, unions' possibilities of industrial action are circumscribed. We cannot expect the Nordic collective bargaining model to be extended to other European countries, because the trade unions in these countries are too weak and show a tendency to become even weaker (Visser 2019). A similar decline also takes place in the Nordic region and this does not facilitate the spread of their system with negotiations between strong social partners. Even though the Council of Nordic Trade Unions weighs heavily in the European arena, other labour organizations still make up the majority; what the Nordic unions can do is essentially to fight for the preservation of a collective bargaining model that so far has served them fairly well.

Notes

1. The first item in Table 3.1 had the response option 'Only to a low degree'. The remaining items presented in this chapter just had the option 'To a low degree'.
2. LO is a short form for *Landsorganisationen*, the large Swedish confederation for trade unions of manual workers.

References

Ahrne, G., and N. Brunsson. 2008. *Meta-organizations.* Cheltenham: Edward Elgar.
Bonin, H., I.E. Isphording, A. Krause-Pilatus, A. Lichter, N. Pestel, and U. Rinne. 2019. *The German Statutory Minimum Wage and Its Effects on Regional Employment and Unemployment.* Bonn: IZA Institute of Labor Economics.
Bruttel, O. 2019. The Effects of the New Statutory Minimum Wage in Germany: A First Assessment of the Evidence. *Journal for Labour Market Research* 53 (10). https://doi.org/10.1186/s2651-019-0258-z.
Caliendo, M., C. Schröder, and L. Wittbrodt. 2018. The Causal Effects of the Minimum Wage Introduction in Germany: An Overview. *SOEP Papers on Multidisciplinary Panel Data Research*, No. 1018. Berlin: Deutsches Institut für Wirtschaftsforschung.
Dølvik, J.E. 2013. *Grunnpilarene i de nordiske modellene. Et tillbakeblikk på arbeidslivs- og velferdsregimenes utvikling.* NordMod 2030. Delrapport 1. Oslo: Fafo.
Eldring, L., and K. Alsos. 2012. *European Minimum Wage: A Nordic Outlook.* Report 2012:16. Oslo: Fafo.
Eldring, L., and K. Alsos. 2015. *Statutory Minimum Wage Regulation in Europe: A Necessary Evil?* Oslo: Fafo.
ETUC. 2007. *Strategy and Action Plan, 2007–2011.* Brussels: ETUC.
ETUC. 2011a. *Draft Reflection Paper for the Winter School: The ETUC Path towards a Future for Growth and Employment through Alternative Integration Policies, Agenda Item 5.* Executive Committee (EC195/EN/5). Brussels: ETUC.

ETUC. 2011b. *Preparation of the Winter School, Agenda Item 7*. Executive Committee (EC196/EN/7). Brussels: ETUC.
ETUC. 2012a. *A Social Compact for Europe*. Brussels: ETUC.
ETUC. 2012b. *Conclusions of the Copenhagen Winter School, Agenda Item 4a*. Executive Committee (EC/197/EN4a). Brussels: ETUC.
ETUC. 2013. ETUC Position on the Social Dimension of the European Union. www.etuc.org/documents/etuc-position-social-dimension-european-union#.
ETUC. 2015a. ETUC Action Programme 2015–2019. Available at: www.etuc.org/sites/www.etuc.org/files/publication/files/ces-congrecs_2015-rapport-uk-ld_def_0.pdf.
ETUC. 2015b. *Paris Manifesto*. Brussels: ETUC.
ETUC. 2018. *ETUC Resolution on Priorities for the Coordination of Collective Bargaining and Wage Policies*. Brussels: ETUC.
Eurofound. 2015. Denmark: Heated Debate About Introducing Minimum Wage. www.eurofound.europa.eu/publications/article/2015/denmark-heated-debate-about-introducing-minimum-wage.
Eurofound. 2019a. *Minimum Wages in 2019: Annual Review*. Dublin: European Foundation for the Improvement of Living and Working Conditions.
Eurofound. 2019b. To Have or Have Not: A Statutory Minimum Wage. www.eurofound.europa.eu/publications/article/2019.
Fernández-Marcías, E., and C. Vacas-Soriano. 2016. A Coordinated European Union Minimum Wage Policy? *European Journal of Industrial Relations* 22 (2): 97–113.
Ferner, A., and R. Hyman (eds.). 1998. *Changing Industrial Relations in Europe*. Oxford: Basil Blackwell.
Furåker, B. 2017. The Issue of Statutory Minimum Wages: Views Among Nordic Trade Unions. *Economic and Industrial Democracy*. https://doi.org/10.1177/0143831X17711769.
Furåker, B., and M. Bengtsson. 2013. On the Road to Transnational Cooperation? Results from a Survey of European Trade Unions. *European Journal of Industrial Relations* 19 (2): 161–177.
Furåker, B., and K. Lovén Seldén. 2013. Trade Union Cooperation on Statutory Minimum Wages? A Study of European Trade Union Positions. *Transfer: European Review of Labour and Research* 19 (4): 507–520.
Georgiadis, A., I. Kaplanis, and V. Monastiriotis. 2018. Greece after the Bailouts: The Impact of Minimum Wages on Wages and Employment. Evidence from Greece. GreeSE–Hellenic Observatory Papers on Greece and Southeast Europe 131, Hellenic Observatory, LSE.

Gumbrell-McCormick, R., and R. Hyman. 2001. *International Trade Union Solidarity and the Impact of the Crisis.* Stockholm: Sieps (Swedish Institute for European Policy Studies).

Gumbrell-McCormick, R., and R. Hyman. 2013. *Trade Unions in Western Europe. Hard Times, Hard Choices.* Oxford: Oxford University Press.

Gumbrell-McCormick, R., and R. Hyman. 2015. *International Trade Union Solidarity and the Impact of the Crisis.* European Policy Analysis 2015:1. Stockholm: Swedish Institute for European Policy Studies (SIEPS).

Hyman, R. 2002. Where Does Solidarity End? *Eurozine*, September 17.

Larsson, B., M. Bengtsson, and K. Lovén Seldén. 2012. Transnational Trade Union Cooperation in the Nordic Countries. *Management Revue. The International Review of Management Studies* 23 (1): 32–48.

Lehndorff, S., H. Dribbusch, and T. Schulten. 2017. European Trade Unions in a Time of Crises—An Overview. In *Rough Waters. European Trade Unions in a Time of Crises*, ed. S. Lehndorff, H. Dribbusch, T. Schulten, 7–35. Brussels: ETUI.

Lovén Seldén, K. 2014. *Europafacklig samverkan. Problem och möjligheter.* University of Gothenburg: Department of Sociology and Work Science.

McGuinness, S., and P. Redmond. 2018. *Estimating the Effect of an Increase in the Minimum Wage on Hours Worked and Employment in Ireland.* Bonn: IZA Institute of Labor Economics.

Nordic Labour Journal. 2015. February. www.nordiclabourjournal.org/i-fokus/in-focus-2015/minimum-wage-for-the-nordic-region/article.2015-02-04.3967575868.

OECD. 2014. *Economic Policy Reform 2014: Going for Growth Interim Report.* Paris: OECD.

Schulten, T. 2008. Towards a European Minimum Wage Policy? Fair Wages and Social Europe. *European Journal of Industrial Relations* 14 (4): 421–439.

Schulten, T. 2014. *Contours of a European Minimum Wage Policy.* Berlin: Friedrich Ebert Stiftung.

Schulten, T., and T. Müller. 2014. Back on the Agenda: A European Minimum Wage Standard. Policy Brief, No. 8/2014. Brussels: ETUI. www.etui.org/Publications2/Policy-Briefs/European-Economic-Employment-and-Social-Policy/Back-on-the-agenda-a-European-minimum-wage-standard.

Schulten, T., and A. Watt. 2007. European Minimum Wage Policy—A Concrete Proposal for a Social Europe. European Economic and Employment Policy Brief, No. 2–2007. Brussels: ETUI.

Schulten, T., T. Müller, and L. Eldring. 2015. Prospects and Obstacles of a European Minimum Wage Policy. In *Wage Bargaing Under the New European Economic Governance: Alternative Strategies for Inclusive Growth*, ed. G. Van Gyes and T. Schulten, 327–359. Brussels: ETUI.

Seeliger, M. 2019. *Trade Unions in the Course of European Integration: The Social Construction of Organized Interests*. London and New York: Routledge.

Skedinger, P. 2008. Sweden: A Minimum Wage Model in Need of Modification? IFN Working Paper, No. 774.

Traxler, F., S. Blaschke, and B. Kittel. 2001. *National Industrial Relations in Internationalized Markets: A Comparative Study of Institutions, Change, and Performance*. Oxford: Oxford University Press.

Vande Keybus, L. 2012. Minimum Wages in Europe: A Strategy Against Wage-Dumping Policies? *Global Labour Column* 86 (February).

Vaughan-Whitehead, D. 2010. Towards an EU Minimum Wage Policy? In *The Minimum Wage Revisited in the Enlarged EU*, ed. D. Vaughan-Whitehead, 509–530. Cheltenham, UK: Edward Elgar.

Visser, J. 2019. *ICTWSS Database. Version 6.0*. Amsterdam: Amsterdam Institute for Advanced Labour Studies (AIAS), University of Amsterdam.

Visser, J., M. Beentjes, M. van Gerven, and V. Di Stasio. 2009. The Quality of Industrial Relations and the Lisbon Strategy. *Industrial Relations in Europe 2008*, 45–72. Brussels: European Commission.

Woolfson, C., C. Thörnqvist, and J. Sommers. 2010. The Swedish Model and the Future of Labour Standards after *Laval*. *Industrial Relations Journal* 41 (4): 333–350.

Open Access This chapter is licensed under the terms of the Creative Commons Attribution 4.0 International License (http://creativecommons.org/licenses/by/4.0/), which permits use, sharing, adaptation, distribution and reproduction in any medium or format, as long as you give appropriate credit to the original author(s) and the source, provide a link to the Creative Commons license and indicate if changes were made.

The images or other third party material in this chapter are included in the chapter's Creative Commons license, unless indicated otherwise in a credit line to the material. If material is not included in the chapter's Creative Commons license and your intended use is not permitted by statutory regulation or exceeds the permitted use, you will need to obtain permission directly from the copyright holder.

4

Revision of the EU Posting of Workers Directive, Social Dumping and Trade Unions' Position

Abstract In 2016, the European Commission proposed a revision of the Posting of Workers Directive and it led to a great deal of debate, with a sharp East–West division in the political reactions. The proposal aimed at eliminating certain kinds of social dumping, arguing that the same work in the same place would get the same pay. Ministers and parliaments in several Central and East European countries raised their voice against the revision. Employers' organizations were generally negative, while the trade union confederations at European level were positive but not uncritical; they wanted a more radical reform. No manifest East–West cleavage became visible in the trade union movement. Even in countries dismissive of the revision, the main labour organizations supported the dominant trade union responses.

Keywords Posting of Workers Directive · East–West conflict · Union attitudes

Introduction

In the summer of 2018, the revision of the EU Posting of Workers Directive (PWD) was adopted by the European Council after more than two years of debate (Directive 2018; Van Nuffel and Afanasjeva 2018). It had then already been approved by the European Parliament. The amendments modified the balance between, on the one hand, EU freedom of providing services and, on the other, its legislation supporting the protection of workers. The debate that preceded the final decisions was quite intense and involved the European Commission, the EU Parliament, EU Member States, the main organizations of the social partners as well as others. The whole issue was very much a matter of social dumping for the trade unions.

The EU rules regarding posting of workers mean that companies from any Member State can win tenders in any other Member State. The original Directive lets companies use lower wages to be competitive, although it postulated a number of restrictions. Still, the arrangement allowed them pretty good chances to increase their market shares and profits, but also to provide more jobs and make jobs more secure for their workers. In this way, there were benefits to reap for both employers and employees, possibly entailing social dumping.

Social dumping is a frequently debated concern in the EU, not least in connection with the enlargement with Central/Eastern European countries. As these Member States generally have lower wage levels and less favourable working conditions than is the case in particularly the Northern, Central/Western and Western parts of Europe, there are differences for various actors to exploit. Notably, a similar discussion took place several years earlier in connection with the entry of Greece, Portugal and Spain as EU Member States (e.g., Bernaciak 2012: 10–12; 2014: 21–23; Voss et al. 2016: 21).

When the European Commission (2016c) in March 2016 proposed a revision of the PWD, questions related to social dumping came into focus. A stated ambition in the proposal was that posted workers should be subject to the same rules as local workers. It can then be asked with whom trade unions in different countries feel solidarity. Is it above all with trade unions in other countries or with their national companies or maybe their home nation? We will examine how various actors and in particular trade unions—both in the sending and in the hosting countries—reacted to the Commission's suggestion of reducing the differences in employment and working conditions between local and posted workers. If the Central/Eastern European organizations regarded the existing system of posting of workers in the EU as advantageous, we could expect them to be against the suggested revision of the PWD. This implies the idea that their interests are best served if they can compete with lower wages, which is presumably unacceptable for unions in other parts of Europe. Thus, the new proposal might pave the way for a conflict or a tension that could be detrimental to transnational trade union cooperation.

The structure of the chapter is the following. First, there is a short description of the phenomenon of posting of workers. Then a section comes on key concepts such as social dumping and solidarity. It is followed by a brief presentation of the first PWD from 1996 and the associated Enforcement Directive (ED) from 2014. After that we outline the main features of the European Commission's proposal to change the PWD. The main research question is what to expect from trade unions concerning this proposal. To provide some background, we give some examples of what has happened in other contexts. Trade unions can have different loyalties and it cannot be taken for granted whether they will be in solidarity with their own companies' opportunities for development, with their own country's economic interests or with trade unions in other countries. The empirical basis for the analysis is the reactions on the proposed revision of the PWD from the political scene and from the social partners. Our focus is on trade unions—due to our concern with the conditions for cross-border trade union cooperation—but we will look at their reactions in relation to other actors' responses. Finally, we summarize and interpret the empirical results and discuss their implications for cross-border trade union cooperation.

What Do We Know about Posting of Workers in Europe?

For several years posting seemed to be a very marginal phenomenon (European Commission 2016a: Annex II; De Wispelaere and Pacolet 2018; Voss et al. 2016: 14–20). Eventually there was some substantial increase but from a very low level. Still in 2017, it was only a tiny fraction of total EU employment.

The first PWD from 1996 contains a definition of the concept of posted worker; Article 2.1 says that the term denotes someone 'who, for a limited period, carries out his work in the territory of a Member State other than the State in which he normally works' (Directive 96/71/EC). The information available is rather uncertain, but one data source commonly used to describe the phenomenon is the information on the Portable Documents A1 (PDs A1), required to establish 'that the holder is properly affiliated to the social security system of the Member State which has issued the certificate' (De Wispelaere and Pacolet 2018: 12). When it comes to social security coordination in the EU, a crucial principle is that individuals 'are subject to the legislation of a single Member State only' (De Wispelaere and Pacolet 2018: 8). The PDs A1 cover somewhat different categories of persons. The most important category includes those who are covered by Article 12 of the Basic Regulation (Regulation 2004). These persons 'are posted by an employer to another Member State to perform work' or they can be self-employed 'who go to pursue a similar activity in another Member State' (De Wispelaere and Pacolet 2018: 12). There is also a smaller, but increasing, category of PDs A1 issued according to Article 13 of the Basic Regulation; these certificates refer to employees or self-employed who work in two or more EU Member States. It should be noted that the number of posted individuals is lower than the number of PDs A1, because a person can have several certificates during a year.

The most recent examination of these data refers to 2017. Data are available for EU Member States, but also for Iceland, Lichtenstein, Norway and Switzerland. In 2017, the PDs A1 were calculated to correspond to 1.2% of total employment in the EU. This meant an increase over the previous year with over 22% and compared to five years earlier with almost 84%. The largest numbers of PDs A1 were issued in Poland and Germany with more than 533,000 and almost 400,000 respectively (De Wispelaere and Pacolet 2018: 21, Table 4). These two countries have been at the top for several years. In third and fourth place we find Spain and Slovenia, each with approximately 190,000 PDs A1. Compared to 2016, Germany had an increase of almost 54% and compared to 2012 its increase was about 64%. The corresponding figures for Poland were roughly 12 and 68%.

On the receiving side Germany and France show the highest numbers, with Belgium as third. The largest net senders (according to Article 12) in 2017 were Poland, Slovenia and Slovakia and the largest net recipients were France and Germany, followed by a number of countries that were close to each other: Austria, Belgium, Switzerland and the Netherlands.

The most interesting aspect for the purpose of the current chapter is to what extent the flows go from low-wage to high-wage countries.[1] In this respect, we focus on information about PDs A1 given out according to Article 12 of the Basic Regulation (De Wispelaere and Pacolet 2018: 27, Figure 8). Notably, during 2017, the clearly largest category of postings happened between high-wage countries. It made up about 40% of the totals. The most relevant flow here—from low-wage to high-wage countries—was the second largest category. It accounted for slightly more than 29% of the total transitions. In third place there was the category moving from medium-wage to high-wage countries (almost 18%). All other flow types were small. There is also information about the PDs A1 issued in 2017 (under Article 12) on sector of activity. Approximately 47% of the postings then occurred within construction (De Wispelaere and Pacolet 2018: 31, Table 9). Two sectors—the service sector and other industrial activities (i.e., with construction excluded)—had roughly 26–27%.

It is more difficult to get an exhaustive picture of the duration of postings, because these data are available only for a limited number of countries. For 2017, we have access to information for 17 countries that issued PDs A1 under Article 12 (De Wispelaere and Pacolet 2018: 34, Table 12). The weighted average was 98 days. There is a wide spread between the countries: low figures for Luxembourg and France (less than a month) and high for Estonia, Ireland, Croatia, Latvia, Hungary and

Finland (over 200 days). It should be repeated that a person can be sent more than once during a year.

Key Concepts

With increasing international competition, the concept of social dumping often gets a central place in the debate. Through the EU enlargement to the East with former socialist countries it has been very much a matter of the East–West relationship. Magdalena Bernaciak (2016: 510) has identified three aspects of this EU enlargement making the fear of social dumping relevant. The first is the opening-up for Western capital to invest in low-wage Central/Eastern European countries, either by moving existing companies or by starting new businesses there. All such investments cannot be described as social dumping, but some of them can. The second aspect is intra-EU mobility of labour allowing people to move from the East to the West and in the new country work for lower pay and under inferior working conditions than others. Finally, companies can temporarily offer services in any other EU Member State, which thus means posting of workers. The PWD sets up certain limits to how wage levels and working conditions can deviate from those in the host country, and the revision of it is about making the rules stricter for posting companies.

We must keep in mind that the phenomenon of social dumping is not limited to a cross-national dimension; it has a much wider application and may very well take place within a country or even within a single company (Bernaciak 2014: 25). This chapter, however, concentrates on the cross-national dimension, due to our interest in the possibilities and difficulties for transnational trade union cooperation.

The concept of social dumping has value-related connotations that are unquestionably negative, but its theoretical meaning is frequently unclear or unspecified. As a consequence, many different interpretations may be implicated. Vague concepts can have a major political and ideological impact, sometimes perhaps precisely because of their lack of clarity. It is obvious that there is a need for theoretical and conceptual clarification. Some authors have taken on this task, for example Bernaciak

(2012, 2014, 2015). In developing her definition, she criticizes several other scholarly uses of the concept. There is, for example, a tendency to confuse lower wages and inferior employment with social dumping and 'unfair' competition. It is moreover common to mix positive and normative elements and to take the standards in high-wage countries as universal frames of reference. Another problem is that many studies are single-case studies, which may not even appear to be related to the same phenomena. In an attempt to 'avoid normative traps and to bring different manifestations under a common analytical umbrella', Bernaciak (2014: 16) defines the key concept as 'the practice, undertaken by self-interested market participants, of undermining or evading existing social regulations with the aim of gaining a short-term advantage over their competitors'.

This is a helpful clarification, but some remarks are justified. It seems that the word 'self-interested' is redundant in Bernaciak's definition; it should be sufficient to say that the actors' aim is to gain advantage over others. In addition, the word 'short-term' also appears to be a dispensable limitation. The argument that speaks for including it is that competition is a relative affair. If someone engages in social dumping, others may soon follow suit with the result that the advantages gained by the first actor simply vanish. This is undeniably a realistic scenario, but there can nonetheless be situations in which dumping companies and companies abiding by norms and regulations exist side by side for a longer period of time. It can still be beneficial for the latter to avoid a 'race to the bottom', for example because of the advantage that lies in maintaining cooperative relations with unions. Likewise, it remains an open question where to draw the line between 'short-term' and 'long-term'. A perhaps more important observation is brought up by Jens Arnholtz and Line Eldring (2015: 82–83). They note that the concept of 'social regulations' in Bernaciak's definition presupposes some kind of norm. Therefore we need to examine how these norms are created and become guiding principles.

A valuable contribution has been made by Annette Thörnquist (2013, 2015) in her analyses of false self-employment (which is rather common, for example, in construction, cleaning, road haulage and certain other industries) as a form of social dumping. Genuine self-employment theoretically means that workers are the owners of their means of production, that they work independently and that they provide goods or services to several clients (Adlercreutz 1964: 6–7). In reality, however, we often find a grey zone in which formally self-employed persons work for only one principal. These persons are subject to conditions similar to those of dependent employees but without having the same rights and protection defined in labour law or through collective agreements. Such arrangements may represent a way of evading certain regulations and hence of lowering labour costs and for that reason they must be regarded as cases of social dumping. Thörnquist (2013: 5; 2015: 414) points out that the method is being used both as a *mode of exploitation* in the capital–labour relationship and as a *strategy for survival* among workers. This is undeniably an important qualification to be taken into account and it is fully in line with Bernaciak's concept according to which different kinds of 'market participants' can resort to social dumping.

Acceptance of a wage reduction or of lower standards in other respects can no doubt be a way for employees to protect their jobs. If their workplace is threatened by downsizing or closure it may be a necessity for continued existence. Another case might be when firms from low-wage countries sidestep rules and norms to win contracts in countries with higher wages; in that way new employment opportunities can be created for their staff. A corresponding reasoning can be applied to job seekers. They sometimes agree to lower wages and/or inferior working conditions than normal just to get a job at all; otherwise they have no income to live on. For example, undocumented immigrants frequently accept much worse conditions than other employees in the country they have moved to, merely to secure survival. Social dumping may thus be a matter of protecting existing jobs as well as a way of creating new job opportunities.

For employers, a simple motive for engaging in social dumping is to increase profits. Such behaviour is associated with two possible advantages for them. On the one hand, if prices are kept the same, it is likely to lead to a greater surplus and, on the other hand, if prices are lowered it is possible to obtain a larger share of the market. In the first case profits can be expected to increase rather quickly and in the second case they will supposedly be higher and/or more secure in the future. In other words, the choice of strategy may be a matter of different time horizons. Furthermore, also for companies, social dumping can be a matter of securing survival. A company threatened by bankruptcy may have an urgent need to cut costs and one way to achieve this is to lower wages and/or to degrade working conditions.

Susanne Pernicka and her collaborators (2015) have argued that stressing economic interests and utility maximization does not make justice to trade unions' social ties with other unions and their commitment to solidarity values and norms. They consider the notion of solidarity 'a universal principle' for trade unions, 'based on the common interests of all workers' (Pernicka et al. 2015: 3). In accordance with these statements it is claimed that we need a neo-institutionalist perspective to pay attention to values and norms and to specify institutional orders and processes (additionally, see Pernicka and Glassner 2012, 2014).

The concept of solidarity is not really discussed in the above-mentioned publications by Pernicka and colleagues. Rebecka Gumbrell-McCormick and Richard Hyman (2015; Hyman 2002) have provided some useful insights into the complexities of the concept by outlining different interpretations of it. The first version takes its starting point in shared identity, which means that people have certain characteristics in common; they can be members of a nation, a tribe or a social class and this may create a sense of belonging and loyalty. The second understanding presupposes awareness that common interests are best taken care of collectively. For trade unions it is evident that employees' interests must be pursued by a collective organization. Solidarity is then founded on both the objective conditions and the perception of these. There is also a third interpretation of solidarity as 'mutuality despite difference', which can be 'a sense of interdependence' or 'an expression of the obligations of humanity' (Gumbrell-McCormick and Hyman 2015: 2; italics removed). This third meaning can be taken to lean towards charity.

Yet another distinction suggested by Gumbrell-McCormick and Hyman (2015: 2) is that between solidarity *with* and solidarity *against*. This implies conflict and may therefore be less relevant for the third concept above ('mutuality despite difference'). In contrast, a typical example of how the conflict perspective can be relevant is when workers feel solidarity *with* one another and *against* employers. Having a clear counterpart—especially if this actor is perceived as antagonistic—can certainly strengthen cohesion among workers.

For trade unions, a core principle is to avoid underbidding among workers. If some workers ask for less pay than others for the same kind of work, it is difficult to make joint demands against employers. Underbidding represents a threat to the possibilities of keeping up wage levels and other employment and working conditions. A measure of solidarity is a key factor for success, but cohesion within and between unions can be exposed to strains, not least in international context where national interests may overthrow other considerations. Divisions between trade unions are likely to be detrimental to transnational trade union cooperation, which is the underlying concern in our analysis. It is important to note that solidarity can go in different directions. The aim of this chapter is to examine a set of circumstances where this might be the case.

The Directives of 1996 and 2014

Posting of workers is allowed according to the four freedoms of mobility in the EU—of goods, services, labour and capital. The freedom of providing services in the internal EU market was ensured by the Treaty on the Functioning of the European Union, but there was a need for some further regulation.

The first directive on posting of workers was implemented by the EU in 1996 (Directive 96/71/EC). We have already seen how the Directive defined the term 'posted worker'. The PWD was aimed at providing a set of common rules for postings and guarantees for 'a level playing field for businesses'. Although its general preamble mentions 'respect for the rights of workers', it was not oriented towards safeguarding that posted workers be treated the same way or get equal pay as workers in the host country (Voss et al. 2016: 22). However, a 'hard core' of rights as defined 'by law, regulation or administrative provision' concerning employment and working conditions must be followed (Directive 96/71/EC: Article 3.1). In the construction sector, and in other sectors if Member States so decided, the hard core could also be defined by 'collective agreements or arbitration awards which have been declared universally applicable' (Directive 96/71/EC: Article 3.1). The rights included rules regarding issues such as minimum rates of pay, maximum work periods, a minimum of rest periods, a minimum of paid annual holidays and regulations on health, safety and hygiene at work as well as non-discrimination.

The regulations of the conditions for posted workers have given rise to a great deal of debate, for example about the existence of 'unfair' competition, fraudulent practices, circumvention of regulations and the difficulties of ensuring a level playing field. Various actors have shown a significant inventiveness in these respects. For example, we find 'letter-box' companies established in low-wage countries just to enable posting of low-paid workers in high-wage countries. In 2014 the PWD was therefore supplemented with the ED (Directive 2014/67/EU), the purpose of which was to combat various forms of abuse and to strengthen the practical application of regulations regarding posting of workers. The ED was not initiated to obtain another definition of the hard core or to remedy the inconsistencies between the PWD and the national social security systems. Its objective was to increase transparency, facilitate controls and guarantee the application of penalties and the collection of fines, should such measures be justified.

The European Commission's Proposal

As mentioned, the European Commission (2016b) proposed a revision of the PWD in March 2016. The ETUC (2010) had then for many years demanded 'a framework of firm and fair rules, combining open borders and adequate protection of workers'. It seems that the Commission was in a similar way of thinking. The existing rules required posting companies to abide by a set of core rights in the host Member State (see further below), in which workers may have higher standards. This means that employers were obliged to pay the receiving nations' statutory minimum wages. Nevertheless, there could be large wage differences between posted and local workers, because the latter were often paid well above the minima. To put it in another way words, wage dumping could become a reality. The Commission's proposal included several measures to change this.

The original PWD was directed to providing a regulatory framework for the transnational provision of services. According to the Commission, it should guarantee fair competition among businesses (a 'level playing field') and respect workers' rights, but the latter objective was not given top priority. The revision was aimed at remedying deficiencies in the existing regulations. In its work program for 2016, the Juncker Commission announced that it would 'present a targeted revision of the Posting of Workers Directive to address unfair practices leading to social dumping and brain drain by ensuring that the same work in the same place is rewarded by the same pay' (European Commission 2015: 8). In a press release in 2016, it was emphasized that the economic and labour market situation had changed significantly since 1996 and with the expansion of the single market, wage differences had increased, 'thereby creating unwanted incentives to use posting as a means to exploit these differences' (European Commission 2016b: 7). It was moreover argued that this development altered the level playing field between companies, with a negative impact on the functioning of the single market. There was also an ambition to improve the PWD's consistency with other parts of EU legislation like the Temporary Agency Work Directive and Regulation 883/2004 on the coordination of social security systems.

The Commission proposed changes in the PWD in regard of three main topics: remuneration of posted workers; rules on temporary agency workers; and long-term posting. Remuneration is a wider concept than the PWD's concept of minimum rates of pay. It includes other elements such as bonuses and pay increases due to seniority. The goal of the proposal was that there should be the same rules of remuneration for posted and local workers, given that these rules are defined by law or by 'universally applicable collective agreements'. Moreover, the Commission suggested that the rules established by 'universally applicable collective agreements' should be extended to posted workers in all economic sectors and not only to those in the construction sector. In addition, Member States would have the possibility of applying the same regulations in case of subcontracting.

Another important part of the proposal was that posted temporary agency workers must be treated the same way as local temporary agency workers. The objective was to create equality between posted and local employees. The current EU legislation required that domestic agency workers be subject to the same conditions as their colleagues in the user company. The proposal thus wanted to extend this principle also to those posted by temporary work agencies from other Member States.

A further suggestion was that postings lasting longer than 24 months should make workers subject to the labour laws of the host Member State. This was already the case according to the social security legislation, but the principle would hence be extended to labour law. For example, after two years a posted worker should be protected against 'unfair' dismissal if the host country has such legislation, no matter whether or not the home country has any such legal provisions.

After more than two years of debates, the revision of the PWD was approved, when both the European Parliament and the European Council adopted it. The revised PWD is to be transposed into national laws by the end of July 2020 and it cannot be applied before that date. The final version is broadly in line with the Commission's original proposal, although some changes were made. One such change was that labour market rules in the host country apply earlier than the Commission had proposed. When a posting has lasted for 12 months, with the possibility of an extension with 6 months, the posting company must follow the labour laws in the hosting country. As noted above, this time limit was 24 months in the Commission's original proposal. We could observe that the revised PWD does not apply to the transport sector, which often has a cross-border character. For this sector the 1996 Directive is still in force. The current chapter is mainly concerned with the discussions that took place after the Commission had published its plan.

It could be expected that the Commission's proposal would encounter different reactions among various actors. To some extent these reactions could be predicted, but it was not so obvious what the answers from trade unions would be. The quotation below illustrates some responses among trade unions in connection with recent EU enlargements and the EU principles of freedom of movement of goods, capital, services and labour:

> While unions in Western Europe focused on the risk of social dumping, their counterparts in the East welcomed unrestricted access to Western labour markets. This is not to say, however, that the latter supported cost-based competition. In relation to the free movement of workers, they insisted that the nationals of new member states should work in EU15 for the same wages as domestic employees. In the mid-2000s, they manifested their anti-social dumping position by joining an EU-level mobilisation drive against the draft Services directive … Justifying their stance, they argued that they did not want to be the cause of 'unfair' competition with fellow workers in the West. (Bernaciak et al. 2014: 70)

A principal rationale behind trade unionism is that workers should avoid underbidding each other. This means that they should make agreements with their employers collectively—through their organizations—instead of each employee doing so individually. Thereby dumping can be avoided, but it becomes more complicated in an international setting when two or more trade unions, often subject to very different circumstances, are involved. What happens when jobs are at stake in different countries? Can conflicts between trade unions then be avoided? By looking at some previous cases, when transnational union solidarity has been put to the test, we can get a glimpse of what might be expected.

Examples of Cross-Border Trade Union Rivalry and Cooperation

A frequently referenced case of social dumping is what happened in Vaxholm, Sweden, in 2004. The Latvian company *Laval un Partneri* had won a contract at a construction site by paying much lower wages than normal for Swedish construction workers. Hence, the Swedish trade union *Byggnads* demanded that the company should sign a Swedish collective agreement. *Laval* then signed two agreements with the parallel trade union in Latvia, still however with much lower pay rates than in the host country. In response thereto, *Byggnads* began a blockade of *Laval*, with some sympathy actions from other Swedish trade unions, and the company eventually went bankrupt. The issue was brought to the European Court of Justice with support from the Confederation of Swedish Enterprise. The Court found that the Swedish unions had the right to take action, but that their actions were not in proportion to the matters concerned. A crucial aspect was also that the unions could not invoke a statutory minimum wage, as Sweden has no such arrangement (cf. Chapter 3 in this book).

There is no need here to go further into the legal aspects of the *Laval* case (for details, see, e.g., Ahlberg et al. 2006; Bücker and Warneck 2010; Woolfson et al. 2010); the point to be made is just that trade unions may end up in viewing social dumping from very different positions. Despite the question at issue, the relationship between *Byggnads* and the Latvian counterpart never became hostile, but perhaps a little cooler. When our research team interviewed an official at the Swedish organization in 2011 (Lovén Seldén 2014: 94), he said that the relationship with the Latvian union had deteriorated for a while at the time of the conflict. This situation had no longer duration. Actually *Byggnads* had for several years provided various kinds of organizational assistance to the Latvians and continued to offer support also after the turmoil created by the *Laval* events. We also made an e-mail interview with a representative of *LBAS*, the Latvian peak trade union. The interviewee emphasized that the cooperation with *Byggnads* had progressed in recent times. Already in 2005 *LBAS* and the Swedish confederate organization *LO* signed an agreement 'to explore the idea of solidarity and to strengthen cooperation between both organizations' (Lovén Seldén 2014: 94, Note 38).

Other Swedish unionists interviewed by our research team in 2011 talked about the *Laval* quartet verdicts functioning as an alarm clock. It meant that it would be necessary for the trade unions to work more actively with unions from other countries and with lobbying in Brussels. The respondents also emphasized the important role of the Swedish trade union office in Brussels and of personal networks and good personal relations. In other words, although the *Laval* experience must be seen as a defeat, it appears to have had some positive effects on transnational trade union cooperation.

An important distinction is that between central-level and plant-level cooperation among trade unions. Bernaciak (2011) shows this by comparing union responses to the EU draft Service Directive and their actions with respect to investments and jobs at GM/Opel factories. The two settings provided very different preconditions. In the first case, it was a matter of contacts between top-level unionists in various countries, whereas plant-level unionists were directly involved in the GM/Opel affairs. Moreover, the issue of the EU draft Service Directive was about outlining a declaration and not about making prompter decisions over investments and jobs. The Directive could no doubt have long-term consequences for work opportunities and living standards, but the rivalries between the GM/Opel factories had an immediate relation to the situation for the workers concerned. In spite of the tough competition in the latter situation, it was possible for the trade unions to establish concrete cross-border commitments and links.

Other examples may also be worth considering. Transnational trade union cooperation is generally more likely to develop in multinational companies (MNCs) (e.g., Arrowsmith and Marginson 2006; Bieler 2005), but this does not exclude the rise of inter-plant rivalries in MNCs making such cooperation difficult. We find illustrations of trade union cooperation and rivalry in the competition between European GM/Opel automotive plants some years ago (Andersen 2006; Banyuls et al. 2008; Bernaciak 2010, 2011, 2013; Gajewska 2008; Pernicka et al. 2015). The company was trying to handle its long-lasting problems with profitability in different ways, among other things, by arranging bidding matches between plants.

One case is the contest over the Opel Zafira model between two GM/Opel plants: one in Gliwice in Poland and the other in Rüsselsheim in Germany (Bernaciak 2010: 124–126; 2011: 36–38; Pernicka et al. 2015: 12). Evidently, the chances for winning were related to workers' claims regarding employment and working conditions. The establishment in Gliwice already had an advantage over the establishment in Rüsselsheim by having considerably lower labour costs. In addition to this, the Polish plant-level trade union—a unit of *Solidarność*—signed a concession agreement with the local management including a three-year wage freeze and lower wages for new recruits. As a consequence, the Gliwice factory obtained the largest part of the production of the Zafira model.

Transnational worker solidarity was definitely put to the test, but cooperation between Polish and German trade unions could nevertheless develop. After the investment had been made in Gliwice, *Solidarność* started to prioritize wage increases and improvement of working conditions and then received support from their colleagues in the West. It was important for the Germans with coordination with the Poles to avoid underbidding. The Polish unionists, for their part, had something to achieve from being cooperative, as in exchange they could receive various kinds of assistance.

GM/Opel's European Works Council (EWC)[2] played an important role in relation to the company's restructuring efforts, to some extent successfully restraining trade union rivalries (Banyuls et al. 2008; Bernaciak 2013: 142–143; Gajewska 2008; Pernicka et al. 2015: 11–12). In 2005, a union committee was set up to avoid 'beauty contests' between five European plants—in Belgium, Germany, Poland, Sweden and the UK—as to the selection for the production of the Opel Astra model. It was called the 'Joint Delta Working Group' and the members soon signed the 'European Solidarity Pledge', demanding fairness in the distribution of investments and assuring that they would not hold separate dialogues with management at the various sites (Bernaciak 2010: 125–126). Still it appears that the British unionists broke the agreement by having negotiations with and making concessions to the Ellesmere Port management (Pernicka et al. 2015: 13–14). Moreover, within the Delta Group, *Solidarność* continued to argue for further resources to Poland on the basis of competitive advantages (Bernaciak 2010: 125–126). In addition, participation in East–West trade union cooperation did not prevent the Gliwice unionists from engaging in a competition with the Zaragoza plant in Spain over another Opel model (Meriva).

As described by several authors (e.g., Andersen 2006: 38–39; Pernicka et al. 2015: 12), there was a similar bidding contest between the GM/Opel factories in Rüsselsheim and Trollhättan, Sweden, concerning the Vectra model. In 2004, together with the European Metalworkers' Federation, the German and Swedish unions rejected this competition in the joint so-called Copenhagen Declaration (EMF 2004). Despite some twists on the thread, this shared effort indicates that trade unions can bring about transnational cooperation even under competitive conditions.

According to Bernaciak (2010: 121–122) 'cross-border union coordination can be regarded as a joint effort to minimize competitive pressure on national workforces, rather than exercising transnational solidarity'. For Pernicka et al. (2015), in spite of some indications to the contrary, the GM/Opel rivalries prove that transnational trade union solidarity can prevail also in highly competitive settings. On the other hand, even if labour actors believe in 'solidarity as a universal principle', they 'still have to accept that their ability (and willingness) to enforce labour cooperation and solidarity beyond national or company borders is rather limited' (Pernicka et al. 2015: 20).

Trade unions are certainly strategic and interest-based actors that are continuously weighing costs and benefits, but their strategic orientations are constrained or facilitated by the structural and institutional settings in which they operate. The generalizability of the examples above may be discussed, but they show that there can be both rivalry and cooperation between unions in different countries. It was thus an open question what union responses could be expected to the Commission's proposed revision of the PWD.

Do We Find an East–West Conflict over the Commission's Proposal?

Following the publication of the Commission's proposal to revise the PWD there were many reactions. Some of the participants in the debate were simply negative, as they found no reasonable ground for the revision. In contrast, others welcomed the initiative but were therefore not automatically uncritical. An overriding question for us was whether we would find an East–West disagreement on the suggested reform. In the presentation of various responses below, we start with the political scene.

Political Reactions

In 2015, the year before the publishing of her proposal, Commissioner Marianne Thyssen received two letters from two different groups of countries (Voss et al. 2016: 51). The senders of the first one were the labour ministers in a group of high-wage countries (Austria, Belgium, France, Germany, Luxembourg, the Netherlands and Sweden). They demanded a significant change of the PWD that should be governed by the principle of 'equal pay for equal work in the same place'. In their eyes it was necessary to create a better balance between economic and social standards and to avoid social dumping. The second letter came from ministers responsible for labour and social affairs in a group of low-wage countries (Bulgaria, Czech Republic, Estonia, Hungary, Latvia, Lithuania, Poland, Romania and Slovakia). It expressed very different arguments. Their contention was that a revision of the PWD would be premature; first, 'a proper assessment' had to be carried out concerning the impact of the ED. Moreover, a revision of the PWD could have very negative effects on the freedom to provide services.

After the publication of the Commission's proposal, the parliaments in the same EU Members States plus Croatia and Denmark showed a 'yellow card' to the European Commission for its suggestion to revise the PWD (Voss et al. 2016: 53–54).[3] Denmark was an exception in this group of countries; its reported motive was just that the reform collided with the subsidiarity principle. The Danish parliament actually emphasized that an important objective would be to ensure equal pay for equal work and that the proposal would help to avoid social dumping. The other ten countries all belong to the relatively new Central/Eastern European Member States and they were all negative to the planned revision, also invoking its incompatibility with the notion of subsidiarity.

A few other parliamentary responses (from Italy, Portugal and Spain) conveyed positive opinions over the Commission's proposal (Voss et al. 2016: 53). It should be noted that the European Parliament had not yet declared a unified view about the proposal, but among the political groups the clearest positions were taken by the Group of Socialists and Democrats and the European Conservatives and Reformists Group

(Voss et al. 2016: 52). The first assembly was positive and the second was negative.

The European Commission responded rather quickly to the yellow card procedure. Its main conclusion in the press release was that the proposal on the PWD revision 'does not constitute a breach with the subsidiarity principle' and Commissioner Thyssen was cited, saying the following: 'We have carefully analysed all arguments put forward by national Parliaments and discussed their concerns with them. All things considered, we have concluded that our proposal fully complies with the principle of subsidiarity and we will therefore maintain it. Posting of workers is a cross-border issue by nature. The Juncker Commission remains firmly committed to the free movement of people on the basis of rules that are clear, fair for everybody and enforced on the ground' (European Commission 2016d).

Briefly summarizing the political reactions to the planned revision of the PWD, we must conclude that the data reveal a rather distinct East–West conflict. It is above all in Central/Eastern European countries that we could observe negative attitudes to the Commission's proposal. Various opinions against the proposal were put forward. It was assessed as reasonable to wait and see what the effects of the ED from 2014 turned out to be. More importantly, there was also a worry that the new Member States would lose competitive advantages and that the freedom of providing services would be circumvented. A more formalistic point of view was that the reform would interfere with the subsidiarity principle. Other political actors—for example, some parliaments in Southern Europe and the Group of Socialists and Democrats in the European Parliament—were positive to the suggested revision of the PWD.

The Social Partners' Responses

BusinessEurope, the main European confederation on the employer side, and a number of national employer organizations in Poland, the Czech Republic, Malta, Lithuania, Latvia, Portugal, Slovakia and Ireland expressed already in 2015, when the European Commission had announced its decision on a 'targeted review' of the PWD, that the revision would go too far in restraining economic freedoms (Voss et al. 2016: 49). There was also a letter sent to the Commission from Nordic employer organizations, worrying about the consequences of the principle 'equal pay for equal work at the same place' for national collective bargaining systems (Voss et al. 2016: 49; italics removed).

When the European Commission's proposal was published, BusinessEurope declared that it could see no satisfactory reason for a revision of the PWD (Voss et al. 2016: 72). The scheme was assumed to damage the freedom of providing services in the European market, by undercutting the competitive ability of companies crossing borders. A further argument brought forward was that the most important task would now be to fight illegal practices and for this purpose the ED was expected to be a useful tool.

Another sceptical organization was the European Construction Industry Federation (FIEC) (Voss et al. 2016: 73–74). It was doubtful to the added value of the proposal. In 2015, it had authored a joint statement with the European Federations of Building and Wood Workers (EFBWW) in which a number of suggestions were put on the table regarding how to avoid abuse. In spite of its distrustful attitude, FIEC found it reasonable that posted temporary agency workers were treated in the same way as such workers in the host country.

The European Confederation of Private Employment Services (EUROCIETT) was yet another organization that disagreed with the revision of the PWD (Voss et al. 2016: 74). It supported the principle of equal pay for equal work as defined in the EU Directive on temporary work agencies, but argued that 16 Member States had already adopted this principle and that it was an option available for everyone. Instead of revising the PWD, the Commission should focus on getting full impact for the ED.

Interestingly, there was also one employer organization welcoming the European Commission's proposal, namely the European Building Confederation (EBC) which represents small and medium-sized enterprises in the construction industry (Voss et al. 2016: 74). The EBC pointed out that smaller companies were generally disfavoured by unfair competition. It thus appreciated a change that could help to eliminate exploitation based on wage differentials.

Turning to the trade union side, we find two organizations to be particularly active in relation to the revision of the PWD: the ETUC and the EFBWW (representing workers in the construction sector, the largest industry for postings). As mentioned above, when the Commission's proposal was published in 2016, the ETUC had for many years advocated that the PWD would be revised and unsurprisingly it thus belonged to the welcoming category of actors (ETUC 2016; Voss et al. 2016: 72). This does not mean, though, that the organization considered the proposal sufficient; it had a series of objections. The ETUC endorsed that the concept of minimum rates of pay would be replaced by the broader concept of remuneration, but at the same time it demanded a clear statement in the PWD that competition with labour costs should not occur in connection with postings. The main argument was furthermore that the proposal contained a too narrow definition of the kind of collective agreements that would be applicable. It was claimed that also sectoral and even company-level agreements must be accepted; otherwise, there would be equal pay only for some posted workers.

Another criticism concerned the Commission's suggestion that when postings had lasted 24 months, national law should be applicable. It is unusual that postings exceed two years, which apparently has to do with 'the restrictions on social security contributions'. In addition, the Commission's proposal left the possibility open for bypassing the time limit. According to the ETUC, the maximum duration of posting should be decided by the host Member State in discussions and negotiations with the social partners.

The ETUC also called for the introduction of a mandatory liability mechanism concerning subcontracting. In regard of temporary agency workers, it was insisted that they be treated in the same way as temporary agency workers in the host country. It was furthermore considered necessary that they had a previous period of employment in that country; if not, they must be treated as being regularly employed there.

The EFBWW had similar comments to the Commission's proposal. It welcomed the extension of the PWD to all sectors as well as the introduction of the concept of remuneration. Like the ETUC, the EFBWW wanted no restriction on the kind of collective agreements that would be valid. This means that the national systems of industrial relations must be respected. On the maximum duration of posting, it was noticed that the 24-month limit was exceptionally long and far from the average.

A fact worth being observed is that the member unions from the Central/Eastern Europe in the ETUC and EFBWW agreed with the positions taken by these confederations. The internal discussions are not made public, but no opposition has been reported. Does this mean that there was no East–West tension in the trade union movement as to the revision of the PWD? Actually, we have found no evidence speaking in favour of any severe such tension. Six main trade unions in the Visegrad group (Poland, the Czech Republic, Slovakia and Hungary) welcomed the Commission's proposal (Joint Statement 2017). They underlined how important it was to create a level playing field for all actors involved. Fair competition for companies and equal rights for workers were deemed indispensable. In particular it was emphasized that 'the paramount principle of equal pay for the same work at the same place must be accepted and included in the Revised Directive as its most essential provision' (Joint Statement 2017; bold style removed). In a separate statement, *Solidarność* (2016) stressed that the proposal went in the right direction to implement 'the principle of equal treatment of employees'. In a later letter—endorsed by a large number of Central/Eastern European unions—on another draft ETUC resolution, it is made clear that the support for the ETUC's position on the revison of the PWD was guided by a future-oriented approach (Solidarność 2019):

> We would like to remind that our organizations, despite pressure from governments and public opinion in our countries, maintained a common and identical [view] with the ETUC's position on amendments to the Posted Workers Directive. It was because we were looking forward. We understood that we could not be guided by short-term gains in form of enabling our entrepreneurs to build their comparative advantage by competing on the basis of lower wage costs.

In searching for other statements on the PWD revision, we have contacted researchers in Poland, Bulgaria and Romania and they have provided information from their respective countries, after consulting with trade unionists. This data collection did not reveal any discontent with the Commission's proposal. There is nothing to indicate that Central/Eastern European trade unions to any significant degree sympathize with the views of the critical politicians and parliaments. It should perhaps not be entirely ruled out that some dissatisfaction could exist below the surface. One relevant question to ask in this context is to what extent posted workers are represented by the labour organizations, given the generally low union density rates in the region.

Trade unions and employers' associations have as a rule responded very differently to the European Commission's proposal for revision of the PWD. The former organizations were relatively positive, whereas—with the EBC as an exception—the latter were sceptical, to a large extent on the same grounds as many of the parliaments in Central/Eastern European countries. When the trade unions put forward criticism, it was mainly because they believed the suggested reform did not go far enough to create equality between posted and local workers. Concerning the questions raised in this article, it is important to notice that the trade unions in those Central/Eastern European Member States where the parliaments sent a yellow card to the European Commission did not agree with their parliaments.

Conclusion and Discussion

The facts examined in this chapter show that the responses to the European Commission's proposal of a revision of the PWD were divided. There was a clear East–West division in the reactions from European politicians. Ministers in nine countries in Central/Eastern Europe and the parliaments in ten countries in the region raised their voice against the revision. Contrary to this, some Southern European parliaments responded in favour of it. In the European Parliament, the Group of Socialists and Democrats was positive and the European Conservatives and Reformists were negative. Regarding the social partners, employers' organizations were typically negative—although with some exception—while the trade union confederations at European level were positive but not uncritical; they argued that the reform did not go far enough. Interestingly, there seemed to be no manifest East–West cleavage in the trade union movement. In spite of strong negative reactions in many Central/Eastern European parliaments, the main labour organizations in these countries supported the dominant trade union responses. Basically, they were all on the same side in welcoming the revision. In other words, a rather predictable employer-trade union pattern comes into sight.

The European Commission emphasized that social dumping had to be tackled. In consequence, it was essential that the same work in the same place would be paid the same. This was a crucial objective of the revision of the PWD, but it does not mean that the implementation of the Commission's proposal will really lead to equal pay for equal work. At best, as the ETUC pointed out, there would be equal pay for some posted workers. One thing to be aware of is that not even all local employees get the same remuneration for the same kind of job. How could it then be possible for posted workers to get the same pay as local workers? Still, it should not be denied that the PWD revision can be a step in reducing differences between posted and local employees. This implies that the competitive advantages that companies from Central/Eastern European countries have in the provision of services in high-wage countries will shrink. The opportunities of competing with labour costs and social dumping will no longer be as obvious as before. It is the restrictions of these opportunities that many Central/Eastern European politicians have protested against. The trade unions in the same nations have not agreed, but instead consented to the opinions against social dumping expressed by the significant European trade union confederations. They made a choice which set them apart from the rather strong sentiments at home. Is this due to self-interest or to their support of wider union solidarity norms?

There is hardly any definite answer to that question. The classification of industrial relations regimes does not give us any guidance in this regard. We can interpret the evidence as an indication of solidarity between trade unions in different parts of Europe. These organizations appear to be in solidarity with each other, which implies that in many Central/Eastern European countries they take a position contrary to the views of the dominant politicians. They have chosen transnational union cooperation rather than the national road for the future.

One aspect to consider is that the statements on the revision of the PWD were made by central-level unionists in the ETUC, the EFBWW and other organizations. These are unionists who may more easily reach consensus, because they do not directly experience the effects of reforms (cf. Bernaciak 2011). It may be simpler for them to adhere to common trade union ideology with its values and norms. We must not therefore completely reject the idea of the effects of solidarity ideology and a neo-institutionalist perspective may help us to see its influence (Pernicka and Glassner 2012, 2014; Pernicka et al. 2015). Nonetheless, we must also take the role of tangible advantages into account, as Bernaciak (2012, 2013, 2015) has reminded us time after time. Cooperation with other European unions is in many ways important for the weak Central/Eastern European organizations. The latter are likely to have much to gain from sharing the experiences of others and many of them receive handy assistance in building up their activities. This is something that they probably find worth keeping. Also, in the long run, more equal remuneration of posted and local workers may be beneficial for all. Competing with lower labour costs can perhaps generate benefits in the short run, but these may become insignificant in a longer perspective. Yet another aspect is the social dumping in Central/Eastern European nations due to the inflow of workers from countries such as Belarus, Moldova and the Ukraine. How should the Central/Eastern European trade unions respond to such developments? They no doubt have several good reasons to safeguard the principle of equal pay for equal work in the same place.

The fact that labour organizations across Europe share the same or similar views on the revision of the PWD has consequences for transnational trade union cooperation. Being in agreement on this issue will certainly facilitate such collaboration within the European trade union movement. The discussion of the revision of the PWD can be said to have been consensus-building. In that sense, it has promoted or confirmed a cooperative climate. As we could see in the previous chapter, not all issues have developed in such a way. There are other challenges for the European trade unions to deal with.

Notes

1. With the definitions used in the report, high-wage countries include Denmark, Luxembourg, Sweden, Finland, Belgium, the Netherlands, Germany, France, Austria, Italy, Ireland, the United Kingdom, Iceland, Lichtenstein Norway and Switzerland. Low-wage countries are Croatia, the Czech Republic, Estonia, Poland, Hungary, Latvia, Lithuania, Romania and Bulgaria. In addition, there is also a medium-wage category: Cyprus, Spain, Greece, Malta, Slovenia and Portugal.
2. From its start in 1996 up to 2012 it was called the 'European Employee Forum' (Pernicka et al. 2015: 9).
3. A yellow card procedure means that the initiator of a legislative change, in this case the European Commission, must reconsider its proposal. It requires one-third of the votes to be effective. The eleven countries represent 22 votes, three votes above the threshold.

References

Adlercreutz, A. 1964. *Arbetstagarbegreppet: Om arbetstagarförhållandet och därtill hörande gränsdragningsfrågor i svensk civil- och arbetsrätt.* Stockholm: P.A. Norstedts & Söners förlag.

Ahlberg, K., N. Bruun, and J. Malmberg. 2006. The *Vaxholm* Case from a Swedish and European Perspective. *Transfer: European Review of Labour and Research* 12 (2): 155–166.

Andersen, S.K. 2006. Nordic Metal Trade Unions on the Move: Responses to Globalization and Europeanization. *European Journal of Industrial Relations* 12 (1): 29–47.

Arnholtz, J., and L. Eldring. 2015. Varying Perceptions of Social Dumping in Similar Countries. In *Market Expansion and Social Dumping in Europe*, ed. M. Bernaciak, 80–96. London: Routledge.

Arrowsmith, J., and P. Marginson. 2006. The European Cross-Border Dimension to Collective Bargaining in Multinational Companies. *European Journal of Industrial Relations* 12 (3): 245–266.

Banyuls, J., T. Haipeter, and L. Neumann. 2008. European Works Councils at General Motors Europe: Bargaining Efficiency in Regime Competition? *Industrial Relations Journal* 39 (6): 532–547.

Bernaciak, M. 2010. Cross-Border Competition and Trade Union Responses in the Enlarged EU: Lessons from the Automotive Industry in Germany and Poland. *European Journal of Industrial Relations* 16 (2): 119–135.

Bernaciak, M. 2011. East-West European Labour Transnationalism(s): Rivalry or Joint Mobilisations? In *Global Restructuring, Labour and the Challenges for Transnational Solidarity*, ed. A. Bieler and I. Lindberg, 33–47. London and New York: Routledge.

Bernaciak, M. 2012. Social Dumping: Political Catchphrase or Threat to Labour Standards? Working Paper 2012.06. Brussels: ETUI.

Bernaciak, M. 2013. Labour Solidarity in Crisis? Lessons from General Motors. *Industrial Relations Journal* 44 (2): 139–153.

Bernaciak, M. 2014. Social Dumping and the EU Integration Process. Working Paper 2014.06. Brussels: ETUI.

Bernaciak, M. 2015. Introduction: Social Dumping and the EU Integration Process. In *Market Expansion and Social Dumping in Europe*, ed. M. Bernaciak, 1–22. London: Routledge.

Bernaciak, M. 2016. Polish Trade Unions and Social Dumping Debates: Between a Rock and a Hard Place. *Transfer: European Review of Labour and Research* 22 (4): 505–519.

Bernaciak, M., R. Gumbrell-McCormick, and R. Hyman. 2014. European Trade Unionism: From Crisis to Renewal? ETUI Report 133. Brussels: ETUI.

Bieler, A. 2005. European Integration and the Transnational Restructuring of Social Relations: The Emergence of Labour as a Regional Actor? *Journal of Common Market Studies* 43 (3): 461–484.

Bücker, A., and W. Warneck. 2010. *Viking—Laval—Rüffert: Consequences and Policy Perspective*. Brussels: ETUI.

De Wispelaere, F., and J. Pacolet. 2018. *Posting of Workers. Report on A1 Portable Documents issued in 2017*. Brussels: European Commission.

Directive 96/71/EC of the European Parliament and of the Council of 16 December 1996 concerning the posting of workers in the framework of the provision of services.

Directive 2014/67/EU of the European Parliament and of the Council of 15 May 2014 on the enforcement of Directive 96/71/EC concerning the posting of workers in the framework of the provision of services and amending

Regulation (EU) No 1024/2012 on administrative cooperation through the Internal Market Information System ('the IMI Regulation').

Directive 2018/957/EU of the European Parliament and of the Council of June 2018 amending Directive 96/71/EC concerning the posting of workers in the framework of the provision of services.

EMF. 2004. Copenhagen Declaration by Trade Union Leaders from IG Metall, Svenska Metall, SIF, CF and European Metalworkers' Federation in Respect of GM Europe Restructuring. Brussels: European Metalworkers' Federation.

ETUC. 2010. *The Posting of Workers Directive: Proposals for Revision*. Brussels: ETUC, March 9–10.

ETUC. 2016. Posted Workers Revision—Equal Pay for Some. Press Release, March 8. Brussels: ETUC.

European Commission. 2015. Communication from the Commission to the European Parliament, the Council, the European Economic and Social Committee and the Committee of the Regions. Commission Work Programme 2016. No time for business as usual. COM (2015) 610 final. Strasbourg: European Commission.

European Commission. 2016a. *Commission Staff Working Document. Impact Assessment.* Accompanying the document Proposal for a Directive of the European Parliament and the Council amending Directive 96/71/EC concerning the posting of workers in the framework of the provision of services. SWD (2016) 53 final. Strasbourg: European Commission.

European Commission. 2016b. Commission Presents Reform of the Posting of Workers Directive—Towards a Deeper and Fairer European Labour Market. Press Release, March 8. Strasbourg: European Commission.

European Commission. 2016c. Proposal for a Directive of the European Parliament and the Council amending Directive 96/71/EC of the European Parliament and the Council of 16 December 1996 concerning the posting of workers in the framework of the provision of services. COM (2016) 128 final. Strasbourg: European Commission.

European Commission. 2016d. Posting of Workers: Commission Discusses Concerns of National Parliaments. Press Release, July 20. Brussels: European Commission.

Gajewska, K. 2008. The Emergence of a European Labour Protest Movement? *European Journal of Industrial Relations* 14 (1): 104–121.

Gumbrell-McCormick, R., and R. Hyman. 2015. International Trade Union Solidarity and the Impact of the Crisis. *European Policy Analysis*. Swedish Institute for European Policy Studies (SIEPS) 2015:1.

Hyman, R. 2002. Where Does Solidarity End? *Eurozine*, September 17.

Joint Statement of Trade Unions of the Visegrad Group on the Revision of Posted Workers Directive. 2017. Press Release, October 20.
Lovén Seldén, K. 2014. Laval and Trade Union Cooperation: Views on the Mobilizing Potential of the Case. *International Journal of Comparative Labour Law and Industrial Relations* 30 (1): 87–104.
Pernicka, S., and V. Glassner. 2012. Horizontal Europeanisation through Trade Union Strategies in Wage Bargaining? A Neo-Institutional Framework. Working Paper, DFG Research Unit Horizontal Europeanization. Oldenburg: University of Oldenburg.
Pernicka, S., and V. Glassner. 2014. Transnational Trade Union Strategies towards European Wage Policy: A Neo-Institutional Framework. *European Journal of Industrial Relations* 20 (4): 317–334.
Pernicka, S., V. Glassner, N. Dittmar, A. Mrozowicki, and M. Maciejewska. 2015. When Does Solidarity End? Transnational Labour Cooperation during and after the Crisis—The GM/Opel Case Revisited. *Economic and Industrial Democracy*. https://www.doi.org/10.1177/014383X15577840.
Regulation. 2004. EC No. 883/2004 of the European Parliament and of the Council of 29 April 2004 on the coordination of social security systems.
Solidarność. 2016. Decision No. 37/16 of the Presidium of the National Commission of NSZZ 'Solidarność'.
Solidarność. 2019. Letter on draft ETUC resolution 'On Promoting Collective Bargaining and Ensuring the Respect of Workers' Right to Fair Pay'. www.solidarnosc.org.pl/aktualnosci/wiadomosci/kraj/item/19067-piotr-duda-do-ekzz-potrzebna-unijna-dyrektywa-o-placy-minimalnej-ma-poparcie-24-central-zwiazkowych.
Thörnquist, A. 2013. *False (Bogus) Self-Employment in East-West Labour Migration: Recent Trends in the Swedish Construction and Road Haulage Industries*. TheMes 41 REMESO. Linköping: Linköping University.
Thörnquist, A. 2015. False Self-Employment and Other Precarious Forms of Employment in the 'Grey Area' of the Labour Market. *International Journal of Comparative Labour Law and Industrial Relations* 31 (4): 411–430.
Van Nuffel, P., and S. Afanasjeva. 2018. The Posting of Workers Directive Revised: Enhancing the Protection of Workers in the Cross-Border Provision of Service. *European Papers* 3 (3): 1401–1427.
Voss, E. in cooperation with M. Faioli, J.-P. Lhernould, and F. Iudicone. 2016. Posting of Workers Directive—Current Situation and Challenges. Brussels: European Parliament's Committee on Employment and Social Affairs.

Woolfson, C., C. Thörnqvist, and J. Sommers. 2010. The Swedish Model and the Future of Labour Standards after *Laval*. *Industrial Relations Journal* 41 (4): 333–350.

Open Access This chapter is licensed under the terms of the Creative Commons Attribution 4.0 International License (http://creativecommons.org/licenses/by/4.0/), which permits use, sharing, adaptation, distribution and reproduction in any medium or format, as long as you give appropriate credit to the original author(s) and the source, provide a link to the Creative Commons license and indicate if changes were made.

The images or other third party material in this chapter are included in the chapter's Creative Commons license, unless indicated otherwise in a credit line to the material. If material is not included in the chapter's Creative Commons license and your intended use is not permitted by statutory regulation or exceeds the permitted use, you will need to obtain permission directly from the copyright holder.

5

Concluding Discussion

Abstract This chapter summarizes the previous analyses in the book in which results from two research projects are presented. Both projects aimed at examining cross-border trade union cooperation in Europe and the conditions for its development. The studies are based on data from different sources: interviews, surveys, documents and direct observations at meetings. They concentrate on actual patterns of cooperative activities, their forms and focuses, and on attitudes among unions to such activities. One aspect that is addressed is what factors labour organizations regard as positive and negative for collaboration. The chapter also sums up how the trade unions have dealt with two vital issues during the last decades: statutory minimum wages and the Posting of Workers Directive.

Keywords Trade union cooperation · Patterns of cooperation · Perceived obstacles/facilitators of cooperation · Statutory minimum wages · Posting of Workers Directive

In this book we have presented results from two research projects. The main object of study in both projects was cross-border trade union cooperation in Europe and the conditions for its development. We have concentrated on its actual activities, on the forms and focuses it has had, and on attitudes among labour organizations to it. Another aspect is which factors unions regard as most important in preventing or promoting collaboration. In separate chapters, our book also deals with two examples of specific issues which have been of vital interest for the trade unions during the last decades: statutory minimum wages and the Posting of Workers Directive (PWD).

The analyses are based on data from different sources: interviews, surveys, documents and direct observations at meetings. The collection of data is described in more detail in Chapter 1. We have conducted two surveys with key representatives of trade unions: one in 2011–2012 and the other in 2015–2016. In addition, we have interviewed a large number of top-level trade union officials. Documents have been utilized continuously throughout the projects. For some time, one of our colleagues in the research team got the opportunity to participate in the ETUC Executive Committee meetings.

A general result from our quantitative analyses is that the theories of (national) industrial relations regimes/regions, sectoral regimes and organizational power resources have supplementary explanatory power. In that sense, they are relevant in a study of transnational trade union cooperation in Europe. However, as illustrated by the two in-depth case studies of national trade union positions on statutory minimum wages and on the revision of the PWD, such classifications are of limited help in explaining what is going on when we encounter both solidarity and conflicting interests in transnational trade union cooperation. In the examples mentioned, the approach has to take more specific issue-related conditions into consideration.

A common classification of industrial relations discussed in Chapter 1 includes five regime types: a social partnership model in Central/Western Europe, organized corporatism in the Nordic countries, liberal pluralism above all in the British Isles, a polarized/state-centred type in Southern Europe, and a transitional or fragmented variety in Central/Eastern Europe. It is a fruitful classification for many purposes, but as always when we reduce a large amount of information to a smaller number of categories there is a risk that intra-category differences are hidden. Sometimes diverging characteristics within regimes need to be highlighted and we have to be careful not to suppress them behind an overall concept.

Unions are more or less powerful in the different regime types. They are strongest in the Nordic region with its organized corporatism and as a rule weakest in Central/East European countries. Union strength can be derived from various sources and four of them are: high membership and a well-functioning organization (organizational power), position in the economy and relationship with employers (structural power), legal rights (institutional power) and alliances with political or civil society organizations (societal power). Strong trade unions frequently obtain their capacity from different sources, perhaps all the four mentioned.

When using union size as a proxy for resources in our analyses, a consistent result was that the larger the union, the more transnational cooperation it could take part in. However, it takes 'two to tango' not only in bargaining with employer organizations, but also in collaboration between unions. Our results indicate that the more resourceful unions are also hampered by the lack of resources among others. The reason can be that the latter have to forgo from participating in meetings and that cooperation may merely take the form of unilateral support rather than mutual exchange. In addition, we should not neglect the effects of insufficient power resources on joint decision-making and influencing the agenda of the ETUC and the ETUFs. One example is how the many but less resourceful trade unions have had problems to raise wage issues on the European agenda, even though there appears to be an interest to do so. As discussed in the analysis of statutory minimum wages in Chapter 3, the Nordic organizations join forces to keep such questions from the agenda.

The differences between regimes stand out rather significantly on their preferences for contentious action and their choice of cooperation through own versus cooperative channels in trying to influence EU policies. The Nordic unions differ significantly from the Central/Western and Southern European organizations by being relatively more restrictive in the former respect. On the choice of channels in trying to influence EU policies, there is a similarly tangible difference between the

Nordics, on the one hand, and the Southern and Central/Eastern European regimes, on the other. The former emphasized the importance of working through their national political parties and their Brussels offices and the latter put much more weight on working through the ETUC and the ETUFs. The labour organizations in Southern and Central/Eastern Europe were also much more ready to transfer authority to these organizations than the Nordic counterparts were.

Sector or industry is another relevant category, above all because some sectors (e.g., manufacturing) are subject to fierce international market competition, while others (e.g., many public and private services) have a more sheltered position with respect to international and sometimes also domestic competition. It is therefore relevant to make comparisons between sectors; it may even generate more exciting and relevant knowledge than comparisons between regimes. A recurrent feature in our analyses was that the cooperation networks in the metal industry were more developed and intense than in the services industry, with construction and transport being somewhere in between these ends. Evidently, there were also important sectoral differences regarding topics of cooperation. For example, unions in construction were inclined to focus on occupational health and safety and migration issues and unions in the metal sector were more concerned with issues of unemployment and employment.

In the beginning of Chapter 2, we presented a classification into four structures of institutionalized cooperation between trade unions: (1) communication, (2) coordination and (3) cooperation networks and (4) meta-organizations, representing different degrees of institutionalization. Actually, all these types exist in Europe and they are in practice intertwined. The most advanced collaborative form takes place in organizations such as the ETUC and the ETUFs, which are meta-organizations, characterized by having other organizations as members. The analysis indicates that bi- and multilateral networking among trade unions is very much related to what these European meta-organizations do. The different overlapping cooperation structures are mutually reinforcing each other.

When examining whether collaboration in national and international meta-organizations, according to the unions themselves, had become more or less important during the last ten years, we found that respondents tended to reply that it had gained greater importance, which was most clear in relation to the sectoral ETUFs. This was confirmed by many trade unions that preferred to strengthen transnational cooperation within their sector rather than within their country for the future. Still, fairly large proportions answered 'same as previously', whereas only few said that the significance of cooperation with any of the meta-organizations listed had decreased.

Another topic dealt with was how trade unions looked upon the European sectoral social dialogue. Large majorities recognized its importance for strengthening transnational trade union cooperation, for influencing EU policies, for negotiations with employers' associations and for meeting workers' interests. Nevertheless, a clear majority of the respondents had doubts whether participation was worthwhile, given the time and resources it takes to be involved in the dialogues. This indicates that many unions have a tight financial situation and are understaffed.

Moreover, a network analysis showed some interesting patterns of trade union cooperation. A most striking outcome was that unions were very much oriented towards other unions in the same region. It was most obvious for the Nordic organizations. Given the discussion of mutual reinforcement between formal meta-organizations and informal network structures, this is not surprising since it is only among the Nordic trade unions that we see joint meta-organizations at cross-national regional level. For Southern Europe a similar but somewhat weaker intra-regional focus appeared. Unions in Central/Western and Central/Eastern Europe presented proportionately more ties with organizations outside their own region, but they still had almost half of their partners internally. Resources and general influence may play a role in these results, but another factor to consider is geographic location. Central/Western Europe has borders with all the other regions in Europe, a circumstance that can be expected to facilitate cross-border contacts.

When scrutinizing the trade unions' concrete cooperative activities, we observed that the most frequent activities were to write statements, petitions or open letters. More contentious forms of action such as overtime bans, strikes and blockades were less regular and it was then common that the organizations collaborated within their own country rather than transnationally in Europe. As regards information on collective agreements, writing joint statements, petitions or open letters and training of union officials, we ran into some substantial transnational cooperation between unions in the same sector as well as between unions in the home country.

The most common topics for trade union cooperation in the home country were employment protection legislation and occupational health and safety. A little bit behind, we found issues concerning wages, unemployment/employment, professional matters and working time. The top topics for collaboration with foreign trade unions within the same sector—all with lower incidence—were occupational health and safety, professional issues, employment protection legislation and migration.

An important question is which factors trade unions view as obstacles to cross-border cooperation. Differences in financial resources among unions emerged as the most important obstacle. Resources are related to union density rates; with larger proportions of employees paying membership fees, the better equipped are the organizations. However, differences in union membership rates were not judged to be a very significant obstacle. We should not because of that underestimate their role. There are enormous differences in union density across Europe, from the high levels in the Nordic region to the very low levels in most Central/East European countries and France. The organizations' financial and personnel resources are negatively affected if only small proportions of employees are members. Such assets are crucial for participating in cross-border cooperation. It is difficult to send representatives to the ETUC meetings, when there are many commitments at home and tight budgets and staffing do not allow the organizations to be fully involved in all matters.

Moreover, an obvious problem is that union density tends to decline almost everywhere in Europe. This development has a negative impact on resources for all the unions hit. It is of course especially problematic when membership is low from the beginning. We should also keep in mind that declining density rates are not only a question of resources; such development may also affect the legitimacy of unions. Organizations claiming to speak for the collective of employees need to have a significant proportion of possible followers as members. On the other hand, the example of France seems to suggest something else; union density in France is very low, but the labour organizations are influential. They are more or less successful in calling for demonstrations and strikes, but collective agreements are frequently extended by law and the law also requires companies with 50 employees or more to consult union delegates about many managerial decisions. France may be exceptional and we must admit that it is impossible to identify a critical point where unions completely lose legitimacy.

The second most important obstacle to transnational trade union cooperation was considered to be the diversity of labour market policies and regulations. This is another way of saying that industrial relations regimes are of great consequence. The fact that we can distinguish industrial relations types is in itself an indicator of the difficulties that cross-border trade union cooperation has to confront. It is likely that collaboration is easier within a regime than between regimes. The results mentioned previously on intra-regional collaboration imply that this argument has some relevance.

It is also noteworthy that cultural factors were not deemed to be very important barriers to cross-border trade union cooperation. This is not to say that they are negligible; they were merely judged as less important than certain other factors. In our interviews with union representatives, we got many vivid examples of how cultural differences can have a negative impact on collaboration, although—on the other hand—some interviewees wanted to downplay their role.

Mirroring these obstacles, we also found that similarities instead of differences facilitated transnational trade union cooperation. The results were largely reversed in comparison with the outcomes on perceived barriers, although in this case there were fewer items for respondents to answer. Similarities in labour market policies and regulations came first in the ranking of facilitators, followed by similarities in occupational interests among unions and union leaders' personal networks and relations. Consistent with the previous outcomes, cultural resemblances were assessed as relatively less important.

As said above, we also examined how European trade unions have dealt with a couple of specific issues. Chapter 3 addresses the question of statutory minimum wages. Most countries in Europe have such arrangements, but the Nordic cluster of nations is an exception, together with a few others. On this topic, there is an unmistakeably deep cleavage in the European trade union movement; some are for legislation, while others are against. In the Nordic region where trade unions are strong and reliant on their own systems of collective bargaining, resistance to minimum wage legislation is especially firm. In most other countries, the labour organizations' views are the opposite. A crucial part of the explanation is that when unions are too weak to secure reasonable wage levels for all workers, legislation can be the way out; it is no wonder if it is then assessed to be an indispensable solution.

Our second survey included six statements, formulated to reflect possible advantages and disadvantages with legislation on minimum wages. Respondents were requested to tell how much they agreed on each of these. Unions in countries with legislation were mostly affirmative of claims that legislation is the best method for unorganized workers to obtain decent wages, that it can impede wage dumping and that it is a necessary arrangement to prevent poverty. Above all the Nordic unions—but to some extent also others in countries without legislation—did not agree very much on these statements. Instead, they were more aware of the potential drawbacks of minimum wage legislation. They tended to think that it undermines the role of trade unions and that it may lead to lower collectively agreed wages. The result was a bit different on an item whether statutory minimum wages would have a negative impact on unions' possibilities of recruiting members. Some of the generally negative Nordic unions agreed with this, but a higher proportion answered 'to a low degree' or 'not at all'. Among the other unions, there was little sympathy for the argument that legislated minimum wages would create recruitment problems for unions.

It is obvious that the European trade union movement is unable to form a united front on this issue. In terms of cooperation, unions that advocate statutory minimum wages can work jointly to reach their goals, but also unions that do not want to have legislation can go together to prevent it. The ETUC has established a compromise formula, according to which national traditions and specialities should be respected. Collective bargaining is treated as the best method to secure decent wages, but in countries where this is not achievable there is a need for legislation. It is thus unlikely that we—on this matter—see a joint effort from the whole European trade union movement. In that respect, cross-border cooperation has apparently encountered a limit. On the other hand, there are repeatedly new initiatives on the question of statutory minimum wages and it remains to be seen what will happen with these.

The other issue paid special attention to in this book is the revision of the PWD. It started with a proposal from the European Commission in March 2016. The main goal was to achieve equal pay for equal work in the same place and to get a level playing field for businesses. The Commission wanted to change the PWD with regard to three main aspects: remuneration of posted workers; rules on temporary agency workers; and long-term posting. It was proposed that remuneration should be introduced as a key concept instead of the PWD's concept of minimum rates of pay. Remuneration would include other elements such as bonuses and pay increases due to seniority. The proposal aimed at the same rules of remuneration for posted and local workers, given that these rules were defined by law or by 'universally applicable collective agreements'. The Commission also suggested that the latter principle would be extended to posted workers in all economic sectors and not only to those in the construction industry. In addition, Member States should have the possibility of applying the same regulations in case of subcontracting. Another part of the proposal was that posted temporary agency workers would be treated the same way as the local equivalents. As domestic agency workers are supposed to have the same conditions as their colleagues in the user company, the Commission wanted to extend this principle also to those posted by temporary work agencies from other Member States. Yet another suggestion was that postings lasting longer than 24 months should make workers subject to the labour laws of the host Member State. This was already the case according to the social security legislation, but the principle would hence be extended to labour law.

The revision of the PWD has now been adopted by both the European Parliament and the European Council—with some modifications of the Commission's proposal. In this book we examine the discussion that followed when the Commission had made its plan public. The opinions really went in very different directions in Europe. Important organizations like the ETUC and the EFBWW welcomed the proposal but expressed that it did not go far enough to achieve the goals identified.

They warned of the risk that the result would merely be equal pay for some workers.

Most interesting was how the Central/Eastern European trade unions would react. The reason why the answer could not be taken for granted was the strong negative responses from politicians in the region. Ministers in nine countries in Central/Eastern Europe and ten parliaments in the same region opposed the revision. In contrast to this, some other parliaments supported it. Thus the trade unions in the East could join either their national politicians or the wider European trade union movement. They actually selected the second alternative or remained silent. We have not discovered any organization that raised its voice against the proposal. Differences in industrial relations regime or in union strength did not create barriers to a common position; the European trade union movement was able to hold together.

The main idea behind trade unionism is that employees should organize themselves collectively to improve or at least defend their employment and working conditions. In this process, they can then prove to be in solidarity with each other and against employers, although there are usually many difficulties and obstacles to overcome. Declining union density rates is one of the problems. The situation becomes even more complicated when organizations in multiple countries—with different economic, institutional and cultural settings—are involved. The trade union movement often speaks in favour of internationalism, but it is far from always clear what this should mean in practice. We must not take for granted that unions in different countries can regularly agree on what they want to achieve. Cross-border trade union cooperation has obtained notable results in Europe, but the question of what is in the best interests of employees frequently remains open. Consequently, trade unions face severe present-day problems and many difficult challenges for the future.

Open Access This chapter is licensed under the terms of the Creative Commons Attribution 4.0 International License (http://creativecommons.org/licenses/by/4.0/), which permits use, sharing, adaptation, distribution and reproduction in any medium or format, as long as you give appropriate credit to the original author(s) and the source, provide a link to the Creative Commons license and indicate if changes were made.

The images or other third party material in this chapter are included in the chapter's Creative Commons license, unless indicated otherwise in a credit line to the material. If material is not included in the chapter's Creative Commons license and your intended use is not permitted by statutory regulation or exceeds the permitted use, you will need to obtain permission directly from the copyright holder.

Index

B

Baltics/Baltic States 40, 42, 68
Banking and finance 21, 22, 45
Brussels offices 53, 54, 123, 144

C

Channels for influencing EU policies 52, 53
   cooperative, 53, 143
   own, 53, 143
Construction 14, 21, 22, 43, 45, 47, 52, 53, 58, 60, 113, 115, 118, 120, 122, 129, 130, 144, 149
Council of Nordic Trade Unions 34, 42, 70, 93, 99, 101, 102

D

Data 5, 19, 23, 39, 76, 92, 95, 100, 112, 131, 142
   documents, 5, 19, 23, 76, 142
   interviews, 5, 20, 76, 142
   surveys, 5, 20, 76, 142

E

East–West conflict 126, 128
Empirical materials. *See* Data
Enforcement Directive (ED) 111, 119, 127–129
European Commission/Commission 2, 3, 5, 15, 16, 18, 23, 39, 40, 110–112, 119–121, 126–133, 135, 149
   proposal of revising the Posting of Workers Directive, 111, 121, 126, 128, 132, 149

European Pillar of Social Rights 2
European Sectoral Social Dialogue (ESSD) 18, 34, 36, 39, 40, 44, 145
  definition of, 18, 145
European Social Dialogue (ESD) 15, 16, 18, 32
  definition of, 15
European Trade Union Confederation (ETUC) 5, 15, 16, 19, 20, 23, 30, 32, 34–36, 38, 39, 42, 47–49, 53–55, 61, 64, 67, 68, 76, 87, 92–99, 101, 102, 130, 131, 133, 134, 142–144, 146, 148, 149
  cleavage on statutory minimum wages, 5, 76, 94, 101, 148
  compromise on statutory minimum wages, 5, 76, 101, 102, 148
  view on the revision of the PWD, 5, 119, 130, 133, 134
European Trade Union Federations (ETUFs) 15, 16, 18, 20, 30, 32, 34–36, 38, 39, 42–44, 47, 48, 53–55, 61, 64, 68, 143–145
European Works Councils (EWCs) 4, 34, 125

F

Factors facilitating cooperation 61
  similarities in labour market policies and regulations, 61, 62, 147
  similarities in occupational interests, 61, 62, 147
  union leaders' personal networks and relations, 61, 62, 147
Focus of cooperation 3, 4, 31, 44, 45, 47, 55
Forms of cooperation 3, 5, 32, 47, 52, 55

G

Government 6, 8, 11, 12, 52, 53, 61, 131. *See also* State

H

Healthcare 14, 21, 22, 45, 47, 58, 61

I

Industrial relations 1, 4, 5, 6, 8, 9, 11–15, 36, 45, 50, 52, 53, 55, 58, 60, 63, 97, 98, 100, 101, 130, 133, 142, 147, 150. *See also* Regimes
  definition of, 8
  European-level, 3, 4, 9, 13–16
Integration 1, 14, 47
  European, 1–3, 16
  negative, 2, 40, 85, 87, 88, 92, 99
  positive, 2, 85, 88

K

Kaitz index 77

L

Labour market policies and regulations 59, 61, 95, 147

Language 45, 60, 61, 63–65, 67
　barriers, 63, 64
　skills, 63, 65
Laval (Quartet) 2
Legislated minimum wages. *See* Statutory minimum wages
Logic of influence 35, 36, 61
Logic of membership 35, 36, 61

M

Metal industry 144
Meta-organization 16, 18, 30, 32, 33, 35, 36, 39, 40, 42, 43, 47, 48, 55, 58, 95, 144, 145
Minimum wage legislation. *See* Statutory minimum wages
Mining 21
Mode of exploitation 116
Multilevel structures of cooperation 31, 47

N

Networks/networking 30, 32, 42–45, 47, 53, 58, 61, 63, 123, 144, 147
　bi- and multilateral cooperation, 31, 32, 35, 42, 43, 144

O

Obstacles to union cooperation 59, 61, 63
　cultural, 63
　differences in financial resources, 59, 60, 146
　differences in labour market policies and regulations, 61, 147
　low priority among union leaders, 59

P

Participation in European trade union activities 49
Posting of/posted workers 14, 110, 111, 114, 118–120, 130, 132, 133, 149
Posting of Workers Directive (PWD) 5, 110–112, 114, 118–121, 126–134, 142, 149
　the European Commission's proposal, 119, 126
　　political reactions to, 127–128
　　social partners' responses to, 128–132
Power (resources) 2, 7–9, 142, 143
　balance, 9, 10
　institutional, 7, 94, 101, 143
　organizational, 6, 7, 30, 55, 101, 142, 143
　societal, 7, 143
　structural, 7, 94, 101, 143

R

Regimes 4, 5, 9, 13, 45, 52, 53, 55, 58, 60, 63, 94, 100, 101, 133, 142–144, 147
　industrial relations, 4–6, 10–12, 36, 52, 53, 55, 58, 60, 63, 100, 101, 133, 142, 147, 150

fragmented (transitional), 10, 11, 142
liberal pluralism, 10, 142
organized corporatism, 10, 12, 142
polarized/state-centred, 10, 12, 142
social partnership, 10, 11, 142
sectoral, 6, 13, 142
Regions 1, 22, 36, 40, 43, 45, 47, 50, 52, 53, 55, 58, 60, 63, 66, 69, 99, 142, 145
Central/Eastern Europe, 9, 13, 20–22, 45, 46, 63
Central/Western Europe, 9, 12, 13, 45, 46
Nordic, 9, 12, 13, 20, 21, 33, 34, 36, 37, 82, 146, 148
Southern Europe, 9, 20, 21, 46
Western Europe, 9, 21, 37
Resources. *See* Power

S

Sector/sectoral 4–6, 7, 11–16, 18, 21, 22, 30, 33, 34, 36, 39, 40, 43–45, 47, 48, 50, 52, 53, 55, 56, 58, 60, 61, 100, 113, 118, 120, 121, 130, 142, 144–146, 149. *See also* Regimes
Social dumping 5, 93, 110, 111, 114–117, 120, 122, 123, 127, 133, 134
Solidarity 7, 42, 69, 79, 94, 95, 102, 110, 111, 117, 118, 122, 123, 125, 126, 133, 134, 142, 150
Solidarność 124, 125, 131

State 6, 7, 11–14, 83, 94
role of, 9, 10, 15
Statutory minimum wages 5, 9, 75–79, 81, 82, 84, 87, 88, 92–95, 97–102, 119, 142, 143, 147–149
arguments against, 82, 88
arguments in favour of, 93
at European level, 5
at national level, 3, 5
cleavage in the European trade union movement, 92, 94, 101, 102
ETUC compromise, 76, 148
Strategy for survival 116

T

Topics of cooperation 9, 31, 55, 144
Trade union 1, 2, 3–9, 11–16, 19–22, 30–40, 42–45, 47, 48, 50, 52, 53, 55, 56, 58, 60, 61, 63, 65, 66, 68, 69, 76, 79, 80, 82–85, 87, 88, 92–95, 97–102, 110, 111, 114, 117, 118, 121–126, 130–134, 142–150. *See also* Factors facilitating cooperation; Obstacles to union cooperation; Union density
definition of, 6, 53
financial resources, 60, 146
power, 2, 6–9
institutional, 7, 94, 101, 143
organizational, 6, 7, 101, 142, 143
societal, 7, 143
structural, 7, 94, 101, 143

readiness to transfer authority to the ETUC, 37
Transport 21, 22, 45, 47, 50, 52, 53, 144

U

Union density 2, 7, 10–13, 80, 82, 100, 132, 146, 147, 150. *See also* Trade union

V

Visegrad group 43, 131

W

Wages 12, 22, 48, 56–58, 77–85, 87, 88, 95–99, 101, 110, 111, 115–117, 122, 124, 146, 148. *See also* Statutory minimum wages

Y

Yellow card 127, 128, 132, 135

The manufacturer's authorised representative in the EU is Springer Nature Customer Service Centre GmbH, Europaplatz 3, 69115 Heidelberg, Germany. If you have any concerns regarding our products, please contact ProductSafety@springernature.com

Printed and bound by CPI Group (UK) Ltd, Croydon, CR0 4YY

23/03/2026

02076447-0013